About the Author

Collin Clarke is a second-generation teacher, who has always had a love and passion for reading and writing. Even as a child, he would craft stories to share with his family, friends, and teachers. He enjoys games of strategy, and is an avid chess and Stratego player. Collin's other interests include running, weightlifting, swimming, traveling, and spending time at the beach. His taste in music is very eclectic. Collin has also always taken a special interest in math, and at one time considered becoming an actuary.

Confessions of a Virtual Teacher:
COVID Edition

Collin Clarke

Confessions of a Virtual Teacher: COVID Edition

Olympia Publishers
London

www.olympiapublishers.com
OLYMPIA PAPERBACK EDITION

A CIP catalogue record for this title is
available from the British Library.

ISBN: 978-1-80439-363-5

This is a work of creative nonfiction. The events are portrayed to the
best of the author's memory. While all the stories in this book are true,
some names and identifying details have been changed to protect the
privacy of the people involved.

First Published in 2023

Olympia Publishers
Tallis House
2 Tallis Street
London
EC4Y 0AB

Printed in Great Britain

Dedication

This book is dedicated to my mother, a veteran teacher and reading specialist, who instilled in me a passion for education, a strong belief in my abilities, and a love for reading and writing.

Acknowledgments

Thank you to my editor, Dani, for all of her guidance and wisdom. Also, thank you to my assistant principal, K.R., for being my guardian angel!

Introduction

In for a Reality Check

I had undergone the full initiation process and was ready to begin my first year of teaching. Or, at least that was what I believed. I was in for a reality check – a *virtual* reality check. I had a six-year-old girl try to wed me. I spent three months leading a group of students who spoke nine different languages. I stood and watched in horror as I witnessed a sixty-pound girl tear a classroom to shreds, beat her aide to a pulp, demolish the principal's office, and then nearly conquer five adults attempting to restrain her. Halfway through my student teaching internship, I was asked to step in and restore order to a classroom full of students who had decided to provide their long-term substitute with a practical social studies lesson on the concept of anarchy. I recall the day that a student with special needs escaped from supervision, stripped himself naked, fled freestyle down the hallway all the way to the cafeteria, climbed into a sink, and then saturated my vice-principal from head to toe with a hose.

When I was younger, my vision of a teaching career and the images that flashed through my mind were a far cry from what I have actually experienced up to this point. Growing up the son of a teacher, I knew *Working for The Weekend* would probably be the worst theme song for the profession because my mother never had a weekend off to gleefully anticipate. My shoulders were sore each week from helping her carry bookbags full of endless piles of homework, which felt like sacks of concrete blocks. I remember all the eight p.m. Friday nights she and I spent together having pizza in her classroom. She always used to emphasize to me how the concept of free time ceased to exist once you entered teaching. When anyone would ask either her or one of her colleagues how many hours their work week entailed, their reply was simple: 'all of them.' My mother always reminded me of this and encouraged me to pursue a field where I would enjoy a lower stress level and more leisure time. I was the classic son who did not heed the advice and counsel of his mother.

When I first revealed my intentions to her to change my course of study, it was a memorable conversation. "You can't be serious!" she gasped. "Are you crazy? You've *seen* how much there is to do for this job! You *know* there's no such thing as free time when you're a teacher! I busted my ass to make sure you could have a happy, peaceful life – not so you could work twenty-four seven, have your blood pressure jacked up every day, deal with tachycardia, and do nothing but homework every weekend!"

"I know it's not easy," I replied. "I've watched you do it my whole life. But you always say how rewarding it is to make a difference for your kids."

"You're right, it *is* – but you don't understand how stressful and overwhelming this job is. Trust me! I've done it for almost forty years, so I know! Don't be stupid! Listen to your mother for once – I *know* what the hell I'm talking about!" my mother insisted.

I could not deny the logic. It was passion that I succumbed to. Out in public, my mother was bombarded with former students approaching her, me by her side. I remember one summer evening when a man in his late twenties approached her while we were in the grocery store together. From behind us, we heard, "Hey! It's you! Do you recognize me?" As my mother turned around, her face lit up.

"Oh yeah! I remember you! How are you? What are you doing with yourself?" she inquired.

"Because of you, I learned how to read. I hated school and thought I wouldn't ever graduate, but you pushed me and forced me to learn even though I fought you every step of the way. I actually just finished my master's degree. I want to say thank you for not giving up on me!" he proclaimed. At the moment, I realized the true extent of the powerful and influential role a teacher plays in a child's life.

The hugs, the thank you notes, and realizing her impact were what she always called 'her true paycheck'. Her love of knowledge and passion for inspiring others were highly contagious.

From a young age, I was certain that regardless of the alternative career path ideas I would often entertain, I would eventually end up in education for at least part of my life. The internal reward I received from helping my classmates and having my peers look to me for help was priceless. My senior year of high school was when I truly contracted the bug for shaping young minds.

Leading an enrichment group of fifth grade young Einsteins every Friday afternoon gave me such a high that could not be matched. I remember how quickly they cracked the secret behind my math mind reading trick, whereas most gullible youngsters would just conclude that I had psychic abilities. "Okay guys, so today I am going to demonstrate proof of extra sensory perception by reading each of your minds." I declared. "But first, I will need you to follow a series of steps in your minds to allow me to connect to your chakras."

"Yeah, all right. Whatever you say," they laughed, rolling their eyes.

"Okay, so first… Think of a number, but keep it to yourself. Now, take that number and double it. Next, add two. Then, divide your number in half." I could see the wheels turning in their brains as they followed each of these steps. "All right, peeps… I'm almost inside your minds. There's just one last step for me to fully connect with you – subtract the number that you originally started with from the number that you have right now. Almost there, almost there… We're connected – your final answer is one!" I confidently declared.

I expected to hearing gasping, see widening eyes and jaws dropping to the floor. Instead, the initial reaction I received from one of my four geniuses was, "Hey! You're not psychic! That's a number trick!"

One girl chimed in, "Yeah! He's right! I figured out what you did. Our final answer is just half of what you told us to add!"

This time, it was my jaw that nearly hit the floor. "Seriously?" I said in disbelief. "There's no way you figured out my secret that quickly!"

"Oh yes, we did!" snickered one of my four, star pupils. Friday afternoons were the highlight of their week, and mine too.

I reflect back with great nostalgia on the probability lesson I implemented with them, where we created edible butterflies to practice with tree diagrams. I brought in a bag of pretzels, three different flavor icings (vanilla, chocolate, and strawberry), an assorted pack of gummy worms containing four different colors (blue, red, green, and purple), and five different flavors of jellybeans. "Your job is to figure out how many different combinations of a butterfly it's possible to make with the supplies I have here," I explained to them. "Each of you is going to build a tree diagram to determine how many different ways you can build your butterfly. Once you solve the problem correctly and I check your tree diagram, you'll get to build your own butterflies and then eat them." Each of their faces lit up as they gasped with excitement. The lesson was a success, and they especially enjoyed the consumption portion of the lesson.

The hands-on projects, the bonding, and the feeling of being loved unconditionally by these youngsters won me over to this crucifying, yet gratifying crusade. This did not mean that I was expecting a fairytale.

I was under no false delusions that the incessant demands placed upon me would be comfortable and painless. I already knew that my daily lessons plans were merely plans – never guarantees. Of course, there would be days when I would feel up to my ass in alligators, especially during report card weekend. Then, there would be the outside of the box kids, the contentious parents, and the performance observations from my administrators which would have me sweating like a pig.

When I committed to joining this profession, I accepted these inevitable truths. I conditioned myself to always expect the unexpected. I still facetiously assert that I am flexible enough to bend, but not to break. Although, when I enlisted myself for this wild ride as an educator, I believed that if nothing else, at the very least, I would get to ride this rollercoaster in a brick and mortar school. My vivid imagination had led me to create many scenes and images of what my first classroom would look, sound, feel, taste, and smell like. However, even my potent imagination lacked the capacity to depict myself teaching a group of students who were not standing or seated in front of me. I never envisioned a virtual reality where I would not only be deprived of personal contact with my students, but also where I would have to manage all aspects of my job electronically. My tool bag was filled with hands-on, paper and pencil, and game style lessons. In no way was I prepared to teach remotely. The field of education is comprised of a variety of different personalities, and mine is certainly unique.

I remember a particular practicum seminar at my university, where my peers and I were seated in a circle of desks. My university supervisor, a woman in her late sixties, about five-foot-three, with short gray hair was seated at a desk directly across from me, in between two of the female students in my group. She adjusted her additional set of eyes, as she glanced down at the list of icebreaker questions attached to her brown clipboard. Then, lifting up her head, she smiled and exclaimed, "We're going to go around the circle. When it's your turn, I want you to share one adjective that *you* feel *best* describes your personality and explain why."

The twenty-two-year-old strawberry blonde seated to my left began, "The word to describe me is definitely optimistic. No matter what any situation looks like at the moment, I believe that when you have a positive attitude it can always be turned around for the better." She batted her eyes and brushed her thick hair to the side.

"Mm, I love it," the supervisor replied, smiling and nodding in approval. The instructor then tilted her head toward me and asked, "So, what's yours?"

"Well," I answered, "I think the best word that describes my personality would be realistic."

"Hmm," she replied with a furrowed brow.

"Would you mind elaborating on that?"

"A lot of people say that when life throws you lemons, you should just make lemonade," I started. "But like I always say —

you can't make chicken salad out of chicken shit, no matter how hard you try!" My supervisor simply shook her head and rolled her eyes. These words of mine have definitely proven tried and true with the great educational experiment we call remote learning.

When the unforeseen zombie apocalypse, also known as COVID, struck the masses in the early months of 2020, I was a teacher with dual certification in both elementary and special education, working as a long-term substitute teacher in a district that I desperately aspired to teach in permanently. This district had a long-standing reputation for their cutting-edge curriculum, supportive administration team, responsive parents, and teacher-friendly policies. The cutthroat competition to secure a permanent position in this district, however, was unreal; clearly something I was not expecting. Veteran educators with years of experience from other districts, and even in neighboring states, would vie for their shot at an interview. It also was not uncommon to find one's resume lumped into, and competing in, a pool of roughly two hundred and fifty applicants for a single position. Although I adored this district, one of their main focuses was the implementation of state-of-the-art technology. I was quite vocal about my anti-technology sentiments. Even to this day, I still attest that technology has a personal vendetta against me. During my practicum and student teaching experiences, technology was the one area that always worked against me. My childhood background consisting of mere books, pencil, paper, an occasional hour of television, and having never played a single video game in my younger years probably contributed to my technological deficiencies as well. One of my favorite jokes was that if I was ever to be subject to eternal damnation, my everlasting torment would involve enslavement as hell's I.T.

person. I could fathom fewer fates worse that would be impossible for me to elude. Therefore, I remember my initially horrified reaction when the term 'remote teaching' rang through my ear drums for the first time.

People automatically make the hasty generalization that since I am a millennial man in my mid-twenties, I must have achieved the highest level of technological proficiency possible. I am accustomed to the surefire reactions of astonishment I receive from those who naively rely on my expertise in these areas. The typical response I hear is, 'You're young, kid. You're supposed to know how to do this techy stuff.' Even during the second half of my undergraduate program, I only earned one C and, of course, this grade was in my prerequisite instructional technology course.

Virtual learning would inherently demand a level of technological expertise that superseded anything I believed myself to be capable of. I faced two simple options: embrace a technological baptism by fire, or desert the profession. Fortunately, my passion and love for the craft triumphed over my inhibitions regarding technology.

The first shutdown in March 2020 placed both my brain and I on the shelf for several months. The emergency version of learning that was rolled out in panic mode at the beginning of the zombie apocalypse crisis was done so in limited capacity. At that time, only full-time, permanent staff were included. Since my position did not fall into this category, I found myself without an occupation for the next several months.

The first two weeks felt like a bizarre, yet much needed vacation; however, the euphoria quickly dissipated. Working with my father on a few small painting and wallpapering projects helped curb some of my boredom. I also invested in a Lifetime

Movie Club subscription, and binged on just about every thriller they had to offer.

During my time on the shelf, I was also recovering from an irritating upper back injury. One-week prior to the mandatory lockdowns, I was rear-ended at a four-way intersection on my way to pick up some fast food after work. The four-hour car trip to my aunt's funeral out of state that I had to make a few days later was a nightmare as well. The stabbing, burning agony kept me up nearly every night for two months. On the positive side, at least this injury did not require me to miss time from work or lose any pay. Those sleepless nights did, however, lead me to the strangest epiphany; I needed to resume teacher mode before my cheese completely slid off my cracker.

The House of Tantrums

(September 2020)

My back finally healed, and my historically long summer break ended at last. I was delighted to receive word that my services would once again be required within the school that had employed me prior to the shutdown. However, I learned that I would not be needed until mid-October.

Fortunately, one humid summer night as both of my hands were buried in my kitchen sink scrubbing pots and pans, I felt my phone vibrate in my pocket and heard the familiar song of my default Verizon ringtone. I reached for the dish towel on the counter next to me to dry off my hands, then reached into my pocket to grab it. Glancing at the screen, I recognized the caller. It was a colleague of mine, my educational diagnostician who was in charge of overseeing special education within my favorite school. I swiped the green telephone icon to answer the call. "Hey there, I may have some good news for you!" she jubilantly exclaimed.

"Oh… Do tell," I replied.

"So," she began, "I have a family who has a child participating in remote learning, and they're looking to hire a certified teacher to work with him." She continued, "They want someone to come to the house each day to sit next to him and work with him while he is online."

My eyes lit up. "A private tutoring situation? Wow! That

seems right up my alley!" I shouted in excitement.

"But wait," she chimed in. "There's a few things you need to know about this kid first."

"Such as?" I inquired. She paused for a moment, sighed, and then proceeded.

"This young man has a lot of emotional needs. He gets upset and flies off the handle very easily," she cautioned me. "He is a really neat kid, though. I love him, and he was always one of my favorites when I used to work in his school. He just needs extra TLC. He struggles a lot in a regular classroom setting. Peer interactions are really tough for him. He has a lot of social skill deficits, and understanding how to behave appropriately toward classmates has been a huge barrier for him. He also really struggles with reading, writing, and math."

"M-hm," I uttered scratching my chin. "So… I take it that there are probably lots of behavioral issues with him?" I inquired.

"Y-yeah," she giggled. "But I think you and him would really connect. Honestly, a positive male role model would be perfect for him and I think that's exactly what he needs!" I hesitated for a moment. Then I asked for the parents' contact information.

I reached out to the young man's mother, and I received an almost immediate response. We agreed to set up a meeting, where I would meet her and her husband, and of course her son, Zeke. As I arrived at the family's front door, I heard ferocious barking and growling. When the boy's father opened the door, I was promptly greeted by a black Labrador Retriever who was not hesitant to pounce on my torso the moment I stepped into the foyer. I had been attacked by this same type and breed of dog in sixth grade, and its sharp fangs had torn the flesh on my forehead. Needless to say, I was already feeling like dashing back out to my car, peeling out of the driveway, and jamming my foot on the accelerator. "Down, girl!" the middle-aged gentleman ordered the hyperactive pet.

I was invited into their spacious living room, where I took a seat on their black sofa that sat facing away from their kitchen and toward a wall with a big screen television that must have been at least six feet long. The mother and father sat on the couch to the right of me, in front of the exterior windows out of which I could see Zeke's private swing set and playhouse. We began with some quick introductions, and then I asked them, "So, tell me a little bit about your son."

They both exchanged a look with one another, giggled, and then Zeke's father proceeded, "Well, he's definitely not a boring kid at all."

"We adopted him from Russia when he was only a year old," the mother interjected. "He's a very sweet kid with a heart of gold. Traditional school is really just not his thing."

"Yeah, that's for sure," laughed her husband. "I'll put it this way – he has quite a thick file in the district office. And I guarantee you, it's in the *front* of that filing cabinet, not the back."

"Oh?" I asked, not fully knowing how to react to these remarks. The mother then shifted the conversation.

"So, basically what we're looking for is someone to sit with Zeke and help him while he does virtual learning," the woman explained. "He needs someone with him to help keep him focused and work with him on each of his assignments. Staying motivated isn't easy for him. He doesn't like being on Zoom, and he needs lots of breaks. He tends to get frustrated and sometimes you'll see him blow up."

"Blow up?" I repeated.

"Well, yeah. There are days when he just goes off the deep

end and he'll shut down completely. Having to deal with a full, structured day of school at home is going to be a really hard transition for him."

"And honestly, we're to blame for that too," admitted Zeke's father. "The last several months, we've kind of just let him do whatever he wanted. We haven't limited his video game time at all, so he's pretty much lived in his own world of fantasy since March. By the way, he's definitely going to want to play video games with you. Are you a video gamer?" he asked.

"Me? A video gamer?" I roared. "I've never played a video game in my life before! I grew up with pencil, paper, and books! I was *lucky* if I had an hour of television each day!" I explained.

"Trust me, ha-ha, you're going to learn *a lot* about video games while you're here," the man assured me. "Enough said, I think it's time for you to meet Zeke," he decided. His wife made an announcement via their Alexa device for their son to report downstairs to the living room, which would be broadcasted in his bedroom. A few moments later, I heard a door slam upstairs and I heard the stomping of feet on the staircase.

A pale, scrawny fifth-grader entered into the living room, his eyes and both hands glued to the iPad he was carrying. Under his breath, I could hear him mumbling, "No, you jump! Stop it! I already got you! There! Take that! How dare you!"

Attempting to gain his attention, the mother said to him, "Zeke, we have a guest." He seemed completely oblivious to his mom's comment and continued his gaming. "Zeke!" his mom loudly asserted. The child looked up at her from his iPad.

"What?" he snapped.

"Zeke, we have someone we'd like you to meet. This guy might be coming to help you when you start school online in a couple weeks. Why don't you sit next to him and introduce yourself?" she suggested.

Zeke plopped down next to me on the sofa. "So, you good at video games?" he started.

"I wouldn't know, because I've never played a video game before," I responded. Zeke's eyes widened and his jaw nearly hit the floor.

"You've never played a video game before? Not even *one?* In your whole entire life?" he shouted in disbelief.

"Nope," I said, grinning at him.

"What's wrong with you?" he demanded. "Are you an earthling? Where have you lived all these years?"

"I never played a video game growing up," I explained. "My mom was a teacher, so I spent most of my time reading and writing when I was growing up. You're lucky your parents let you have all this gaming equipment in the house," I assured him.

"You're going to learn to play video games!" he asserted.

"And you're going to learn that video games aren't the only way to enjoy your leisure time," I gently replied. That day, since I had planned to spend some time getting to know Zeke and begin establishing a rapport with him, I packed a board game in the trunk of my beige Honda Civic.

My game of choice was Stratego. Stratego has been my favorite board game since childhood, and I hoped that perhaps I could interest Zeke in this as well. Each opponent plays with the same set of pieces: a flag, bombs, and different ranking soldiers who possess different abilities. We set up our pieces within the first four rows on each of our battlefields. I ran through the rules with him. "The object of the game is to capture my flag, so you need to do everything you can to protect it. Higher ranking soldiers take out lower ranking soldiers. If two soldiers of the same rank collide, the attacker has the advantage. Each piece can move forward one space either vertically or horizontally, except your rank two pieces which are scouts and can move an unlimited number of spaces. Your three soldiers are miners and can diffuse bombs. Your S ranking piece is your spy and he's basically useless, except for the fact that he can take out your highest ranking ten piece *if* the spy attacks first. Also, you've got soldiers, not navy seals – they can't swim across the lake squares on the game board," I explained. "So, do you want to play?" He smiled from ear to ear and nodded his head rapidly up and down.

Zeke thoroughly enjoyed playing the game, although I had ultimately annihilated his entire battlefield within the first twenty minutes of playing. "Hey, that's not fair! You can't do that!" he would argue whenever I took out of one of his men. I found it particularly hilarious when one of his pieces would strike a bomb and I would holler, 'boom', at the top of my lungs, causing him to jerk backward in his chair. I have perfected my poker face during my near two decades of experience of playing this game, so he was clueless as to when I was in danger of him defeating one of my higher-ranking pieces nor did I even let an ornery grin slip across my face when I knew he was about to march his army straight into a trap that I had set for him. *Progress,* I thought to myself.

After I captured Zeke's flag in Stratego, we headed into the sun room which was adjoined to the living room, where there was an air hockey table. "I love air hockey!" I beamed. "How often do you play?" I asked Zeke.

Of course, he replied, "I don't play air hockey much. It's not as cool as playing video games." I convinced him to play a round of air hockey with me, with the bargain that if he played one round with me, I would venture into the video gaming world for the first time in my life to play a round of his favorite video game with him. This sealed the deal.

Predictably, I was victorious in air hockey. That meant it was time to fulfill my end of the bargain. I collapsed onto the black sofa facing the big screen, where Zeke joined me. He handed me a video game controller. I took one look at this bizarre device which had unfamiliar features such as a joystick, which I had never been exposed to before. I examined the controller, squinting as I tried to focus in on the specific buttons. "How do I use this thing?" I asked him. Impatiently, he turned his face to me.

"Look, it's not hard. Use this to make your character move," he instructed, pointing to the joystick in the middle of the controller. "Push this button to jump," he said, pointing at a green button on the side of the device. "Can we just start now, or do you have to keep asking more questions?" I did not want to push my luck with this child, since it was only my first time meeting him and his family.

"I'll figure the rest out as I go along," I falsely assured him.

About seven minutes into our round of the video game, Zeke began shouting at me, "You have to jump to grab that package! It'll make you rich! Jump! Jump! Grab it!" When I failed to jump and grab the object in time, Zeke tossed his video game controller and threw his hands up in the air. "What's wrong with you? Why didn't you do what I told you and grab that damn package?" he bellowed at me. Zeke's mother, who was working in her office which was to the left of the living room, overheard this comment and came trotting into the living room where we were playing.

"He's new to this game. You have to understand, he's never played a video game before. He's not an expert like you are," Zeke's mother explained to him.

"Well, I'm trying to help him and you're ruining our game!

Why did you have to come in here? Why couldn't you just mind your own business and leave us alone?" he shouted at her. He rose from his seat, kicked the coffee table in front of us, and then threw himself face down onto the floor. He screamed and pounded on the carpet for several minutes, until his mother finally laid down next to him.

"It's okay, baby, let's just take some deep breaths and calm down," she coaxed. Zeke continued pounding and sobbing for about ten more minutes. Finally, he began to quiet down. Zeke's mother lifted him up, brought him over to the couch, and sat down, holding him in her arms. "I'm so sorry you're upset, honey," she cooed. "He didn't mean it. He's never played a video game before, he didn't know any better, sweetheart," she said, referring of course to me. I was amazed at how she seemed to be subtly hinting that somehow, my ignorance of the gaming world made me culpable for the boy's temper tantrum.

After Zeke calmed down and she had sent him back upstairs, she sat back down in the living room with me. "So, can you be available to start the Tuesday right after Labor Day when Zeke starts back?" she asked.

"Yes, that will work. But I should give you a heads up that my principal has a long-term position for me in October, so I can only work with Zeke for a month," I forewarned her.

"Sure, we completely understand. Do you happen to know an approximate date in October?" she inquired. Although I knew that I was not tentatively scheduled to begin until the middle of that month, I did not want to lead her on to this in the event that I needed an early exit excuse.

"I really have no clue. You know how it is – maternity leaves are always very fluid. You never know what babies might decide to do," I reasoned with her.

"I totally get it," she said. "Just try to give us some notice when the time comes."

"Oh, I most definitely will," I promised, a strained smile on my face. We agreed on a wage of seventeen dollars per hour for my services. I would quickly come to regret not advocating for at least twenty. One of the reasons I agreed to the lower compensation was because, as part of the agreement, I would not begin until ten a.m. each morning. Since mornings have always been my Achilles' heel, I was over the moon with this proposition.

I reported to my new private tutoring position on my first day with a positive attitude and a determination to make an impact on Zeke. I entered the home and approached him where he was sitting at the kitchen table in front of the family's laptop. I pulled out a chair and seated myself directly to the right of him, angling myself perfectly so that I was just close enough to see everything on his monitor but at the same time the camera would not pick my face up on Zoom.

The three teachers were having students complete an icebreaker. "So, everyone, you're going to draw a sketch of yourself based on your interests and hobbies," one of the teachers instructed. "The directions are on the first slide. For example, if you prefer working alone to working in a group, then color your eyes blue. If you like math more than you like reading, color the hair of your sketch brown. If you like reading better than math, color the hair blonde. You guys get the idea. Alrighty, go ahead and take about twenty minutes on your sketch and then upload it." I figured that this was a student friendly, introductory activity and I assumed that Zeke would take to this task with ease.

"So," I said to him, "let's look back at the first slide where the directions are, so we can figure out how to color your sketch in."

"This is the stupidest thing ever! I don't understand why I have to keep wasting my time with shit like this! I want to go play video games!" he shouted.

"Zeke," I began calmly, "I understand you've gotten used to having a lax schedule these past few months, but you're in school right now even though you're at your kitchen table. I'm happy to help you with everything, but we really need to work *together.* Are you willing to do your part with me?" I asked gently.

"No!" he screamed even louder. "This stuff is so hard, so pointless, and so fucking stupid! I don't need it, and it doesn't help me! I don't care about school, school hates me, and I'm dropping out the first chance I get!" insisted Zeke.

"Zeke, you really need to calm down," I coaxed.

He then picked the laptop up off of the table and threw it across the other end of the kitchen. Next, he stood up, flipped his chair over onto the floor, and stormed into the living room, howling and bawling all the way. My young firecracker hurled himself face first onto the red sofa next to the window, kicking his feet and punching the pillows. His mother came dashing in from the dining room to the rescue. "What's wrong? Is everything okay?" she asked softly. He uttered a few unintelligible syllables, while continuing to cry and scream.

After almost half an hour, he finally began to settle down. "I hate Zoom class! It's so boring, it's a waste of time! I don't care if I fail! I'm not going to do it!"

"I understand you're frustrated, Zeke," his mom empathized. "You can just lay here until you feel better." She grabbed one of the pillows on the couch and handed it to her son. "Here," she said. "Just punch this until you get all of your anger out of your system." He took his mother's advice, and began his boxing match with the poor, helpless pillow. "There you go, sweetheart!" encouraged his mother. "Doesn't that make you feel better?"

"Aaaaaaahhhh!" he roared.

As Zeke's mom headed toward the dining room, she gestured for me to follow behind her. "Please don't take it personally. He's really a sweet kid. School just frustrates him. It's really hard to keep him motivated. Hopefully, he'll get better in a few days," she said, with a strained smile on her face. I simply smiled and nodded, not saying a word. I jumped in my car and peeled out of their driveway that afternoon, as soon as my workday was over.

The rest of the week was similar. I felt knots in my stomach each morning when I hopped into my car to drive to Zeke's home, my hands sweating as they held onto the steering wheel. I felt as though I was being strangled by the collar of my shirt. The next few weeks seemed as though they would be impossible to manage. I brainstormed some clever ideas over the weekend, and tried to assure myself that implementing them on Monday would improve my work environment.

I strolled into what I now referred to as *The House of Tantrums* on Monday morning, determined to break the vicious cycle. In my small black arm bag, I carried a few small tools that I hoped would enable me to reach Zeke: a yellow piece of tag board, a composition notebook, and a copy of the novel *Hatchet* by Gary Paulsen.

I approached Zeke and sat next to him at his kitchen table, just as I did every other day. I slipped the yellow piece of tag board out of my black bag, and set it in front of him. "We're going to try something cool, Zeke," I explained to him. "Have you ever heard of a point card before?" I asked him. He nodded his head sideways. "So, basically what it is, is like a reward system," I clarified. "Here's how this is going to work. You are going to have an opportunity to earn points each day for every assignment you complete, every ten minutes you stay focused, and for every half hour you last without a meltdown."

Of course, his first question was, "Well, what do I get if I earn points?"

"That's the exciting part," I continued. "If you reach at least fifty points by the end of each day, I'll stick around for an extra twenty minutes just to play video games with you."

He just stared at me for a minute, then asked, "You mean it?"

I nodded my head. "I sure do."

He looked up, thought for a moment, then finally said, "Okay."

"Great." I smiled.

I then revealed the copy of *Hatchet* that I packed. "You and I are going to read this novel together," I told him. It's a fictional survival story about a young boy, not far from your age, who gets stranded in the wilderness and has to learn how to survive."

His eyes widened. "Oh, that's sounds cool!" he replied excitedly.

Next, I held up the black composition notebook. "For each chapter that we read together, you're going to write a journal entry as if you were Brian, the main character."

"Oh, come on!" he protested vehemently. "Writing is the worst!"

I giggled and replied, "It won't be as bad as you think."

For the next two or three days, I noticed a minor improvement in his behavior. The number of emotional outbursts were reduced from four or five per day to only about two or three. He was beginning to willingly complete more of his assignments, and I was beginning to wonder if I would begin to dream about video games at night. However, progress was short lived.

One morning, I was sitting with Zeke at his kitchen table working with him on an activity that involved multiplying the dimensions of a box to calculate the number of total objects it could hold. "So, Zeke, how we can figure out the length—" I was abruptly interrupted.

"I don't know!" he exclaimed, folding his arms and lowering his head.

"Okay, Zeke, how about we count the number of units together and I help you come up with the right multiplication equation," I suggested.

"No, I don't want to! Shut the hell up and get out of my face!" he demanded.

My jaw fell open in shock. "Zeke, I'm your teacher, not your personal punching bag!" I replied sternly. This further escalated his emotional crisis.

"I hate you! You suck, and you don't understand me! You just torture me and make me do this shit that I don't understand! You should just leave, because I don't want you here any more!" He picked up his pencil, and threw it straight at my torso. He picked up the family's laptop and hurled it onto the floor, then charged into the living room. Naturally, his mother came running out of the dining room – where she was working – to come coddle him.

For nearly two hours, he wailed, screamed, and would not budge off the living room floor. To finally get him to deescalate, the queen of the *House of Tantrums* finally said to him, "You don't have to do Zoom for the rest of the day, baby. Just take some deep breaths, it's all going to be okay," she cooed softly. She then looked over at me and said, "You can still hang around if you want and get your hours of pay."

Zeke's father was working from home that day, and heard the entire scene. Before I left, he emerged from his office to speak to me. "So, that was quite an encounter you had with our boy today, huh?" he chuckled.

"Um, yeah, you could say that," I replied sarcastically.

"Oh, that was nothing. He got suspended once for hitting one of his classmates with a chair and telling him that he was going to kill him by bashing his mother-fucking brains in. On the bright side, at least Zeke wasn't *too* mad at you, because he didn't threaten to kill you," joked the father.

"Oh wow, that's so comforting," I sarcastically responded.

"Aww, don't take it personally. Zeke's a great kid," he assured me.

His wife chimed in as well. "We've had a lot of people interject their two cents about how we should discipline our child, and how we should parent. They've told us that we ought to restrict his privileges, take away his video games, and send him to his room when he doesn't behave the way he should. People also tell us that we're not doing him any favors by letting him get away with whatever he wants, and that he's going to end up in jail one day. But you know what – we don't give a shit about what they think. He's *our* son, and we're going to do things our way. He just needs love, and you know what – punishments are useless. They don't work. They're nothing but total bullshit," she reasoned. It was abundantly clear that I would not be supported in my quest to hold Zeke accountable for his actions and utter disrespect toward me. With a couple of weeks left in this private tutoring role, I decided to just survive day by day to the best of my ability.

Reading *Hatchet* for half an hour each afternoon once Zeke was finished with Zoom school proved tiring as well. Although I would read the majority of the chapter, getting him to read one or two paragraphs felt like performing oral surgery. Each time Zeke would get stuck on a word, he would utter a loud grunt and smack himself in the head with his copy of the book. An attempt at getting him to produce a journal entry with two complete sentences was seldom successful.

In the chapter where the pilot in the story was having a heart attack and Brian was forced to land the plane on his own, I asked Zeke, "So, how do you think you'd feel if you were on a plane, the pilot was having a heart attack, and you were only twelve or thirteen years old, and you had to land an aircraft all by yourself?" Zeke simply shrugged his shoulders. "Would you feel scared or nervous?" I asked.

"I guess so," he mumbled.

"I know I'd be," I remarked. "So, Zeke, how about you write a couple of sentences pretending to be Brian and describe how you're feeling about having to land a huge plane all alone with a dead guy sitting in the cockpit."

"I don't want to write any stupid sentences!" he hollered.

"All I'm asking you to do is write two complete sentences. You're a fifth grader. It's not unreasonable for me to expect this of you. If you can write two complete, legible sentences, I promise we'll play a round of your favorite video game together as soon as you're done," I said to him. He hesitated for a moment.

"Fine," he agreed. It took him twenty minutes to write two complete sentences. I had to return his work to him multiple times, leading to more grunting, growling, and smacking himself in the head, but nevertheless he prevailed through the task.

There was never a moment of peace within the *House of Tantrums*. Even during Zeke's lunch break when he would spend time outside on his swing set, relaxation was nearly impossible.

As I attempted to consume my food, the black Labrador retriever would climb up onto the table. When I tried to lift her down, she would whimper and whine, and quickly climb back up onto the table. Her greedy face kept shoving its way onto my plate, and guarding my lunch became a daily battle.

I employed a new strategy before I unpacked my lunch each day. As Zeke would log off for his mid-day break, I would let the dog out the sliding glass door in the kitchen. I would then unpack my meal, sit down, and attempt to enjoy a moment of peace and quiet. However, the dog was able to witness me dining through the sliding glass door which was directly across from the kitchen table. She would bark and howl, which I would ignore. The persistent canine would then resort to backing up, running forward, and slamming her whole body into the glass at full force. She would repeat this several times.

Finally, the queen of the *House of Tantrums* came running to the rescue. She slid the door open, and allowed the thieving beggar to flood back into the kitchen. She reached down into her pot cabinet, and yanked out a black frying pan. She opened the fridge and pulled out eggs and milk. She cracked several eggs into the frying pan, added milk, salt, and pepper, and topped the dish with cheese. She plated up the meal, then served it to the dog.

It was no wonder that Zeke had learned that tantrums and fits were an effective way to manipulate his parents. Observing how the dog was able to practically run the household empowered the young fifth-grader to replicate these behaviors. The end of that painful month-long sentence finally came, and I was ready to flee the *House of Tantrums*.

Although there were still more weeks until my long-term position would officially begin, I informed the king and queen of the *House of Tantrums* that my final day would be 2 October 2020. "I have to begin transitioning to my new role, starting next week," I told them. "Before the teacher's maternity leave starts, I need to spend a few days with her in the virtual classroom to learn the routines, get acquainted with the students, and review the curriculum."

"Oh, that makes sense, I guess," Zeke's father said in a melancholic tone.

"Well… I suppose we'll have to start looking for a few people on Care.com to take your place." The mother sighed.

"That's a good site! I'm sure you won't have any trouble finding someone on there!" I cheerfully interjected.

On my last day, the parents invited a young lady who expressed interest in the position to join us for an interview. I was also asked to attend the interview since, "I could offer valuable insight on Z." The doorbell rang. A young, twenty-one-year-old blonde-haired, blue-eyed girl standing at about five-foot-four stepped forward into the foyer. We headed for the living room, and took a seat. I was curious about her background.

I casually asked her, "Are you an education major?"

She giggled and responded, "Oh no, I actually have a degree in communications." She must have noticed my furrowed brow, because she then added, "But I've worked with kids a lot over the years."

Over the years? I thought to myself. *You have fewer years than I do!*

"I've had lots of babysitting experience, and I've been pitching in at different summer camps over the past several years," she continued.

"Oh," I responded, casually nodding my head. It was not my place to critique this girl's qualifications or professional background. I was just intrigued by the fact that the family would resort to hiring someone with no background in the field of education. Although she had childcare experience, I doubted that someone without professional training and skills would be up to the task of managing an exceptional child such as Zeke.

She shadowed me for the entire day as I worked with Zeke. Fortunately for the king and queen of the *House of Tantrums*, she did not witness any of Zeke's typical conniptions or emotional outbursts. Zeke even wrote his journal entry for *Hatchet* that day without complaining or destroying his pencil. The young girl was hired to take my place, more than likely for a significantly lower rate of pay.

Her compensation was no concern of mine. I was now able to devote my energy to preparing for my transition into my new role as a long-term substitute in third grade at my school of choice.

I will admit, however, that experiencing virtual learning from the student's side of the screen definitely provided me a different perspective going in. Zeke was but one example of a child who struggles with the remote learning format. Keeping my students engaged online and motivating them to want to participate in virtual school would be a challenge, especially those with exceptional needs like Zeke. My next role would provide me with more practical, hands-on experience working with children with special needs.

Baptism by Fire

(October 2020 – January 2021)

I was molded into the educator I am by being tossed headfirst into 'shituations'. I sat through my share of teaching methods courses, college seminars, and tedious lectures where I consumed countless liters of Pepsi and Coke, while completing all the required abstract coursework I needed to pacify my university and state licensure board. However, all the hours invested in my mandatory textbook readings, term papers, and exam preparations failed to negate one reality. It is common knowledge that every diamond is nothing more than an ordinary lump of coal that demonstrates the ability to withstand extreme pressure. Without practical experiences, I was still just a lump of coal. Challenging shituations are what truly reveal a teacher's strengths and weaknesses. That magic date in October was upon me, and I found myself back to working for the same school in a long-term position.

The Saturday morning before I was scheduled to report for my first day in third grade, my phone rang a little after ten a.m. I yawned, stretched, and reached over to my nightstand to grab my phone, my eyes half open. "Hello," I mumbled.

"Hey there!" I quickly recognized the voice. It was my principal. "So, you know V is out as of Monday?" she asked.

"Yup, I'm all set and ready to roll first thing Monday morning," I managed to utter. She knew I had joined their Zoom meeting for three days of shadowing.

"Okay, and you're aware that you're in the building with your in-person group on Mondays and Tuesdays, correct?" she confirmed.

"Yes, ma'am," I answered, my voice beginning to sound more like normal.

"Phew, this is gonna be a shit show," she laughed. "I don't know how elementary kids are going to manage five hours in the building without being able to basically move at all," she remarked. The typical student day was six hours; however, all elementary schools in my district operated on a shorter schedule where students were dismissed one-hour earlier to allow custodians additional time for cleaning and sanitation, and teachers additional time for adjusting to an entirely new format of learning.

Since the number of deaths and cases of the virus had slowed somewhat at that point, a hybrid format of learning was implemented. The class was divided in half, into two cohorts. One cohort came in person twice per week for face to face instruction with a teacher, and the other group attended live instruction via Zoom twice per week. On the days that the live cohorts were receiving their instruction, the other cohort would complete independent work with no access to a teacher. Wednesdays were the one exception. Initially, the entire class would meet on Zoom for live instruction for half of the day; however, my school district generously and graciously determined that allowing teachers to utilize the full day on Wednesdays for planning, collaboration, grading, and data entry would best serve the district. This essentially meant students would only receive two lessons per week in each core subject, as opposed to five. This would prove to be interesting in my case. I was just grateful to have a sense of normalcy return to my life, albeit a limited one.

Entering this new assignment, my ultimate objective was to make the greatest impact in the lives of my temporary students for the duration of the time which they would have me. This duration would turn out to be four months.

I was placed into a two-teacher inclusion classroom, with a significant proportion of students identified with various learning disabilities. Of the approximately twenty students in this class, roughly seven received special education services. "V gave you a copy of the IEPs before she went out, didn't she?" my co-teacher asked.

"Yeah. There in the Google doc she set up for me last week. I've glanced at them, but I still have to finish reading the last few from cover to cover," I replied truthfully.

"Well, you better learn 'em and memorize 'em quick. These parents know their shit, and they're going to be watching us like hawks," she warned.

An Individualized Education Program (IEP) is a serious matter. One of my special education college professors gave the same speech, week after week. "An IEP is a *legal document*," he emphasized. "If you have a kid with an IEP, they are entitled *by law* to receive those specific special education services and accommodations, *exactly* as they're stated, to the *letter*. If it says they get thirty minutes per week of small group instruction on math word problems and you only give them twenty-nine minutes, your ass can be sued by a parent and you'll lose your license. If you don't dot every 'i' and cross every 't', you can kiss your career in education goodbye." This blunt warning has always resonated with me.

Fortunately, V prepared my first week worth of lesson plans

for me in advance. This allowed me to focus on reviewing and familiarizing myself with each of my IEPs. One of the science plans that were left for me involved a Nearpod activity. Nearpod is popular among many educators as an efficient platform to share lesson presentations with students, take polls, and administer quizzes and assessments with a class.

There is one lovely feature of Nearpod, that I discovered on the spot. Nearpod lessons can either be set in teacher-paced mode or in student-paced mode. When taking a quiz or answering a set of questions, student-paced mode allows students to proceed at their own speed. The teacher-paced mode forces students to remain on the exact same slide as the teacher, and advancing my slides forward meant advancing students' slides forward as well. Since this activity was created by the regular teacher, it did not occur to me to check the settings nor test the activity in advance – an oversight that I would quickly come to regret when carrying out this Nearpod activity over Zoom.

During this activity, I assigned my students to different breakout rooms on Zoom. Breakout rooms are a great way to work with small groups of students or an individual student at one time, especially if they require extra help with a specific concept or if they have an accommodation entitling them to have a small group setting while completing an assignment. The downside to breakout rooms, however, is that if a large number of students encounter a problem with an assignment, hopping between different rooms can be difficult. Meanwhile, students become more and more impatient, frustrated, and disengaged while waiting for their teacher to enter their room. This is what I was about to experience.

In my first breakout room, I was working with a small group of students. I was attempting to read the question and passage aloud to them, when I saw flashing on my screen: 'a student in room three asked for help.' So, I told my group, "Pardon me for a second, friends, I'll be right back." I bounced into the other breakout room. I was greeted by a confused parent.

"Hi there. My son's trying to move on to the next question, but it won't let him," she explained.

"Hmm. That's odd," I replied, puzzled. I clicked forward to the next question on my screen.

"What about now?"

The parent glanced at the screen. "Okay, it's on the next question now."

I saw another help request for a different room appear on my screen.

I jumped into the next breakout room. A grandparent of one of my students with special needs was standing behind the little girl's chair. The elderly woman leaned over the chair and glanced directly into the screen. The little girl's eyes were red, with tears streaming down her face. "My granddaughter is very frustrated. She's trying to get your activity to work, but clearly there's something wrong on your end. She shouldn't be responsible for completing an activity that doesn't work." Before I even had a chance to finish responding to her, I received another help request.

It was yet another room containing one of my students with special needs. His mother stood before the screen with a distraught expression on her face. "My son is extremely frustrated and angry right now," she stated. "Something was malfunctioning with the activity, and he couldn't get it to work. He just ran out of his room screaming, biting his arms, punching and kicking himself."

Finally, my co-teacher and I closed down breakout rooms

and terminated the activity. Thankfully, it was a Friday. All of the parents and students would have an opportunity to forget about the incident over a weekend, and it also bought me time for reflection and troubleshooting.

By the beginning of my second week, I was beginning to acclimate to the routines of the class and the 'new normal' of in-person 'hybrid' learning. My face to face students on Mondays and Tuesdays only left the classroom once during the entire school day, when it was recess time. To line my students up, I had to call them one by one. Each child had to stand at least six feet away from one another, and maintain that distance until they arrived outdoors. The line formed a giant S that stretched clear from the door at the far end of the classroom to the door at the opposite end.

I never thought that there would come a time when I would rejoice over recess duty each day; however, COVID is irrefutable evidence that there truly is a first time for everything. It was the one of the only opportunities, aside from bathroom breaks, where I was allowed to lower my carbon dioxide infested face diaper and actually inhale fresh oxygen.

After recess when students came in for lunch, there was no exception that would allow them to move from their seats. My co-teacher and I sprayed down each child's desk and delivered paper towel to them for sanitation, prior to consumption of their meals. Lunches were delivered to the classroom, and they were placed on a table directly next to the main entrance door at the front left of the room. Since students were not allowed to leave the room to go to the cafeteria, one of the related arts teachers would come to provide us with lunch coverage, which would allow us to leave the room for our lunch break if we elected. A large trashcan was available in the room, and the teacher in charge of supervising the students during lunch would roll it around to each individual to collect their waste at the end.

October turned to November and this meant the end of the first marking period was imminently near. The final two weeks of the marking period was also the time where data had to be collected in order to determine whether or not our students with IEPs had made adequate progress toward the special education goals.

Collecting student work samples remotely was always an intuitive process. We had to gather and maintain data separately for students' IEP goals. We were required to maintain binders for each student that contained evidence and supporting documentation. My co-teacher had a sophisticated system in place for executing this process. "Hold a picture of your work up to the screen. Higher. A little more to the right. No, your other right. Now, back a little bit. Hold it nice and still. Please don't move it. Just two more seconds. Perfect!" Click! I would then take the screenshot and paste it on the same word document with the problems and directions. Then, I would print everything out and file it into the students' binders. Although data collection was dreadful, managing to provide accommodations to these students throughout our daily instruction was made easier, all thanks to Schoology, which is my personal favorite platform.

Schoology allows me to create folders where I can paste announcements, create, post, and grade student assessments, and send my students instant messages. It also has many neat features that allow me to meet the needs of my students who require specific accommodations. Since I had six or seven students in this class with unique needs, I found these features very helpful. One particular feature I frequently utilized was the audio recording feature. I recorded assignment passages, questions, and directions in advance for my students who struggled with reading fluency. Most of my students' IEPs explicitly stated that they were entitled to have all materials, including math word problems read aloud to them. I had one particular student with a print disability which prevented him from reading and comprehending texts, and this feature saved my co-teacher the time of having to step away from the rest of our students to serve as his human reader.

I loathed having to test each of my recordings and being forced to hear the sound of my own voice played back to me. I also wanted to cringe on our two in-person days when I would be circulating around the room and was subjected to the torture of listening to my audio recordings reviewed by the students over and over. Not that anyone is a huge fan of hearing their own voice, but I especially detest hearing mine. By the end of my tenure in this position, I was even considering seeking out a vocal cord operation.

November marked the most contentious IEP meeting that I have ever experienced in my young career. It was for a student I dubbed 'The Wizard.' I felt that The Wizard was befitting for this student due to a number of reasons.

In The Wizard's Zoom background, she often was visible laying sideways against a blue blanket, her eyes closed and her mouth hanging open. One day my co-teacher and I were taking notice of her on camera. "This is ridiculous," my co-teacher asserted. "She literally sleeps all day long. I tried waking her up in a breakout room. I called and called her name, and she wouldn't budge. I'm so done with this shit."

"Ah, The Wizard is probably in Oz with Dorothy right now," I joked. "She isn't in our class right now. She's not in Kansas either."

My co-teacher roared with laughter, nearly falling backward in her chair. "You're a mess!" she hooted.

There was also the day where we saw in her background that there were two hands rubbing and massaging her scalp, as The Wizard was yawning and struggling to keep her eyes open. "Are you seeing this?" my co-teacher asked. "I guess she gets in-home spa service," she scoffed.

"Oh no. You know what – she probably grants three wishes out to anyone who rubs her head," I snickered mischievously.

"I'd be scared to put my fate in her hands," my co-teacher laughed.

"So would I," I agreed.

When solving math problems, The Wizard had a unique gift or so she thought. It was her solemn belief that she had special powers in mathematics that would allow her to defy any and all logic to reach a solution. I could not make rhyme or reason out of any of the steps she took in approach to a problem. I called her work "magic math," because I could never wrap my brain around how she came up with what she did. My favorite joke was that my virtual magic marker that graded her assignments was powerful enough to prevail against any powers that The Wizard had at her disposal.

There was a "flex time" block built into the virtual school day, which was intended to be utilized for providing additional intervention to students, working with small groups of students to fulfill the requirements of their specialized instruction needs, or to collect data to monitor progress toward IEP goals.

The Wizard had a math word problem solving goal, where she had to be able to identify the correct operation, set up the equation correctly, and solve the problem accurately. One afternoon when I was working with her in a breakout room, I asked her to solve the following word problem:

Carol got a paycheck in the amount of $650 placed in her bank account. She had to take $150 out of that to pay for her electric bill. How much money did Carol have left afterward?

I read the problem aloud to The Wizard, and even highlighted the key clues in the problem for her. I then asked her to solve. I sat for a few minutes, waiting for her to work her magic. Finally, she emerged with an answer. "1000," she uttered.

"How did you come up with that?" I asked, puzzled.

"I plused it," she answered.

"You what?"

"I plused it," she repeated.

"Why did you add for this problem, instead of subtract?" I inquired.

"To get the answer!" snapped The Wizard.

"Okay – but if Carol is paying a bill, is that putting more money in her pocket or taking money out of her pocket?" I tried reasoning with her.

She rolled her eyes and replied, "It doesn't matter as long as Carol pays the bill."

In frustration, I smacked my hand against my forehead. I am a firm believer in refusing to be an enabler. So, I continued on, "Okay… If you have to pay for something, like a candy bar for instance, are you getting richer by spending money on it?"

She did not answer.

"Well… are you?" I asked again.

She shrugged her shoulders. "I just make my parents pay for it."

I rolled my eyes, and sighed in defeat. The Wizard managed to stall and ride out the full half-hour block of time without any further progress.

The day of The Wizard's IEP conference, my co-teacher had a family emergency. Luckily, my principal and fearless leader came to my side and I was not cast to the wolves without a shepherd. The meeting began with the parents barking and spewing their rage toward another staff member in the meeting who provided speech therapy services to their young child. "Why haven't you been meeting with her to provide services?" they demanded. "She is entitled to get what she needs!"

"Well, I have attempted to pull her three times so far this year, but she is either asleep or not logged onto Zoom," the lady replied.

"It's your responsibility to communicate to us and reschedule a different time!" the wolf pack hastily retorted.

In defense, she explained, "I sent you two emails the other week, I didn't hear back from you."

"Emails?" snapped the mother. "I run a business! My husband and I both work every day! We don't have time to check our email on a daily basis! I don't get why you people don't understand that we need a phone call, not an email!"

My principal then had to intervene. "Email is the standard acceptable form of parent communication from staff in our district, and it is the primary method school officials will continue to use when communicating with you in the future," my fearless leader asserted. "Our speech therapist will continue to schedule dates with you to ensure that your daughter receives a remote speech session," my principal politely assured them.

"Yes. And please know that my next outreach to you will be through email, because that's how I communicate," the speech teacher stated. Next, the two snarling wolves turned their attention toward me on Zoom and I could feel their icy glares piercing my skin like knives.

I knew I was not too much further down their shit list. "Sir, we thought we made it crystal clear to you that we don't have printer access at home. What part of that is tough for you to understand, and why do you keep requiring my daughter to print everything out?" the father demanded.

Before I had the opportunity to unmute my microphone and testify in the hot seat, my guardian angel intervened. "Students are *not* required to print materials," my principal calmly clarified. "The students just need to download the math materials, show their work on a sheet of paper, and simply upload a picture of their work." On this particular day, my principal happened to have her granddaughter in her care, who was innocently playing in the background.

"What's all that crazy noise in your background?" the mother shouted at her. "Whoever that is making that racket in your house is too distracting! You need to either mute yourself or keep that girl quiet!" I sat behind my monitor with my jaw hanging down in disbelief. We all rejoiced when the meeting concluded. I later learned that after that the full-time teacher returned, the wolf pack had raised a strong objection to having the principal attend any future meetings pertaining to her daughter. I just chuckled at this insanity. There were two extremely valuable lessons I learned from my encounters with The Wizard and her family.

Facing entitled parents is a reality whether a student is in person or virtual. Many families of virtual learners, this simply being one example that I have encountered so far in my professional experience, do not accept any accountability for their child's learning. They do not take seriously the commitment that they make to ensure that their children have the tools, the structure, and the environment at home to be successful with remote learning. Since their child is not attending school in-person, these parents are not burdened with having to drive students to school, walk them to the bus stop in the morning, or pick them up or be ready for their return in the afternoon. They also view distance learning as an opportunity to avoid other essential parental duties including ensuring that they are properly groomed, appropriately dressed, maintaining healthy hygiene, or observing a healthy sleep schedule. However, it is even worse when the child from one of these families has special education needs, as was the case with The Wizard.

The Wizard was in special education, and required what is known as a 'B setting,' meaning that she required more intensive services outside of the general education classroom than most other students with disabilities. Attending regularly both mentally and physically, in a state where she was able to focus and learn, was extremely vital to her chances at success. Her entitled parents, as opposed to allowing us to form a partnership with them for the sake of their young child, instead decided to point their fingers at us. Blaming the educators and the school district was far easier than executing their parental duties. To make matters worse, these parents had countless safeguards provided to them by special education laws that made it nearly impossible for my co-teacher, my administration, or myself to enforce any type of accountability. If we attempted to disseminate a truancy letter for the days that The Wizard was either offline or asleep on Zoom, or if we attempted to forcefully move her to a hybrid learning format with two days per week of in-person instruction, the wolfpack would not hesitate to file a vicious lawsuit. Of course, the suit would make outrageous and false claims that services were being denied and that the school system was derelict in its duty. Despite the fact that ultimately these claims would never be corroborated, simply the headache and publicity of the threat of legal action would be deemed more than sufficient cause by the district to placate the parents. A family who enrolls a child with a learning disability in remote learning and has no vested interested in that child's education, is doing the greatest disservice to them. The Wizard was practically left stranded up Shit's Creek without a paddle.

As Thanksgiving was directly over the horizon, my co-teacher and I received a visit from the school guidance counselor. "Hello, loves," she beamed, a bright smile stretched across her face. "So, I've just got to give you a heads up. That friend who's on your roster who hasn't been here since the beginning of the year is coming back tomorrow. He was just released from that mental health facility," she explained. "I'll be sending you guys some more info about that shortly. Have an awesome day, friends!" she said cheerfully, skipping back out of the door.

Shortly after becoming acquainted with this new friend, I determined that he too deserved a nickname, just like The Wizard. I branded him 'Sergeant Schultz.' Sergeant Schultz is my favorite character from the old television show *Hogan's Heroes* that was filmed ages before my time. Schultz was known for feigning ignorance. His most common catch phrases included, 'I see nothing, I hear nothing, I know nothing.' This student mimicked quite a bit of Sergeant Schultz's behavior with a learned helplessness.

His favorite tactic was pretending as though directions or instructions were never communicated to him. On several occasions, Sergeant Schultz even denied having conversations with me that took place the day prior. One day, he raised his hand and summoned me over to his desk during our flex time block. "I can't log into Dreambox. I don't know how," he whined.

Dreambox is a math software that my district heavily utilizes, which provides students with specialized lessons that are presented as games, animated adventures, and challenges.

"All right, I'll show you," I replied. I stood next to the student and navigated him through step by step how to access his account. I placed a yellow sticky note in the upper right-hand corner of his desk that contained all of the steps, as well as his log in information. "This will stay here on your desk, and it'll be here for you tomorrow too when you log in," I explained.

The next day, he once again gestured for me to walk to his desk during the last block of the day. "What am I supposed to do?" he asked, puzzled.

"We just went over the directions three times, and it's written on the board – you're on Dreambox right now," I reminded him.

"I didn't hear you say that," he argued.

"It was also up on the board over there," I reiterated, pointing to the giant dry erase board hanging up on the front wall to the left of the smart board.

"What board? I didn't see anything on a board," he replied, flabbergasted.

"Just go ahead and log in now," I instructed him. "If you forget how, you can look back at the sticky note I put on your desk yesterday."

Sergeant Schultz flashed me a puzzled look, his eye brows furrowed. "What sticky note?" I realized that the note from the previous day was not on his desk.

"The one I took the time to write directions out on and attach to your desk yesterday," I insisted impatiently.

"I have no clue what sticky note you mean. I don't see anything," he proclaimed.

"Hmm," I said sarcastically.

"Maybe, you've got a case of amnesia. If you have amnesia… I… I really just don't think it's safe for you to be playing outside at recess… Could be dangerous for you today, so maybe you ought to sit next to me while all your classmates play," I suggested.

"No, that's no fair!" protested Sergeant Schultz. "I probably just lost it by accident. P-please give me another one! I-I'll be careful with it this time. I won't lose it! I swear to God!" he pleaded.

"Okay, I will – but, this time you're going to take a screenshot of it with your iPad, so you don't *lose* it again. I'm going to take a picture of it with my smart phone too, just in case your amnesia returns again," I remarked. Sergeant Schultz loved to play his role on a daily basis – at least on the few days that he actually reported for duty.

Sergeant Schultz was chronically truant. On some of our in-person learning days he would pop in. However, Sergeant Schultz was missing in action on every single remote learning day. Given the fact that the majority of school days were still virtual at this point, he fell far behind and became more convincing in character.

In fact, he was almost mistaken for that identity. One day, the student teacher intern who worked in my placement classroom under the supervision of my co-teacher was charged with writing names on the students' desk for seating assignments. As she approached him, marker in hand, she began writing his first and last name on his desk. After she inscribed his last name, he glanced up at her with a look of confusion. "Wait a sec," he spoke. "My last name isn't 'Schultz'," he claimed.

Tapping the marker on his desk, she replied, "Umm, y—yes, it is."

"No, it's not!" he insisted. "That is *not* my last name!"

"Look dude," she continued, "your last name is *Schultz*. And so that's what I've written on your desk." As she walked away, Sergeant Schultz's jaw hung wide open.

The intern approached my co-teacher and I. "What's his deal?" she asked, subtly pointing to Sergeant Schultz.

"What do you mean?" I asked. "Well, he's acting really strange. I wrote his last name on desk, and he just started arguing with me. He's like, 'my last name ain't Schultz.' And I was like, 'um, yeah it is and that's what I've written on your desk, because that *is* your name'." My co-teacher and I were silent for a moment. We turned and looked at one another. Then, we faced her again and burst out in riotous laughter, my co-teacher nearly doubling over onto the floor. The students curiously glanced over to the scene the three of us were making over in the front corner of the room.

I gestured for the intern to follow me to a private space in the back of the room. "Look," I started, barely able to maintain a straight face. "I nicknamed him that. Sergeant Schultz is a character from an old television show, *Hogan's Heroes.* His famous phrase is 'I see nothing, I hear nothing, I know nothing.' I figured this fit our friend well, since he always feigns ignorance."

"Oooohhh," exclaimed the intern. "I get it now."

For the remainder of the day, the three of us were unable to look at one another without bursting into a fit of laughter. "You're a mess," my co-teacher giggled.

"Agreed," I conceded.

The days of December leading up to winter break were never dull. The last few weeks of December prior to the beginning of break, our school district decided to temporarily resume a fully remote learning format until January, due to the rising number of corona virus cases. This meant that the holiday gift exchange would have to take place over postal mail as opposed to in-person. I sent a small gift to my principal in an envelope. My co-teacher had a gift shipped to her as well.

When I returned to work after the New Year, I noticed a bizarre change in my principal's behavior toward me. One day, as I passed her in the hallway, I smiled and waved. She looked at me is if she had seen a ghost, awkwardly waved back, then turned her back and scurried away in the opposite direction. For the next few days, when I would greet her, she would abruptly nod without uttering a single syllable to me. I had absolutely no clue as to why she was acting so aloof, as she and I had had a strong rapport for several years.

Then, one afternoon as I was walking my class back upstairs after recess was over, I spotted my co-teacher and my principal outside my classroom door chatting with one another. As soon as I approached, I heard my principal whisper to her, "Oh, here he comes," as she bent forward laughing. Before I entered the room, my principal tapped me on the shoulder and said, "Hey, I need to talk to you for a sec. The student teacher can watch the class for a minute." She and my co-teacher exchanged another look and began doubling over with laughter again.

Finally, I interrupted and asked, "Okay, don't keep me in suspense here. What the hell's so funny?"

"I owe you an apology," declared my principal.

"For what, exactly?" I asked, scratching my head.

"Well now, you see, I received a gift in the mail – a pretty outrageous gift. I knew you told me to keep me eye on the mail for something from you, so when I got this crazy thing, I couldn't believe that you would send me something like that," she explained.

"Send you what… exactly?" I asked again. My co-teacher began cracking up again, bending over and nearly collapsing to the floor.

"I got an inflatable male nut punching sack shipped to me as a gift," she revealed. "Before your ornery partner over here told me today it was from her, I just assumed you did it, because you've given me some pretty interesting gifts before. I was avoiding you, because I felt too awkward. I didn't know how to approach you. I mean, what was I supposed to say – 'thanks for the sack'?"

"That was definitely *not* me," I assured her. "I know I've sent you some memorable gifts before, but c'mon… Booze, sure. A nut sack, though? I don't think that's even up to my level of intriguing gifts," I exclaimed. My co-teacher was still in amusement over the fact that I was blamed for this outrageous gift.

"Ha ha ha!" she roared. "I think it's so damn hilarious that she blamed *you* for that! That's the best part!" I just shook my head.

"Yeah, yeah, yeah. Joke's on me," I admitted.

From that point on, my principal felt comfortable embracing me and greeting me. Meanwhile, a plan to implement the next phase of hybrid learning known as 'Hybrid 2.0' was already underway. A large black Logitech camera had been installed in each classroom, including mine. At the beginning of January, training was offered to all teachers.

Our instructional technology coach, who I refer to as 'the geek squad' because of his roots as a former IT associate for Best Buy during his college days, led this training over Zoom. He held the large, black, square-shaped remote that controlled the camera. "These buttons control the angle. If you want to zoom in on yourself or change the angle in which the camera is facing, let's say to capture what's on your smart board, just press this," he explained, demonstrating with his finger on the buttons. "And this one, is the mute button," he continued, pointing at a red button on the remote. "If you push this, you'll mute the Logitech camera and none of the students who are watching your class from Zoom will be able to hear what you're saying," he explained. The geek squad then dived further into the significance of this technology in our classrooms.

"So, starting the on last week of this month, Hybrid 2.0 is going into full force. That means on Mondays and Tuesdays when you have your in-person crew, your group that is virtual on Thursdays and Fridays will also be zooming in from that camera and participating in your live instruction on Mondays and Tuesdays as well now." Although the entire staff was muted, I had no doubt that many sighs were being uttered at this news drop.

The last week of January of 2021 was the week when V, the teacher on maternity leave who I was standing in for, was scheduled to return. "Well, I guess I'm going to dodge the bullet of that new Logitech system for right now," I joked with this co-teacher.

"Lucky you," she sourly replied.

"Maybe not," I suggested. "I'm going to be forced to use it in my next long-term position."

By the time my tenure in third grade had ended, my principal already had an idea of another potential opening for me. "So, I may have another spot coming open soon that I can slide you right on into." she said. "But it's not official yet. I should be able to tell you more in about a week or two." she clarified.

"I get it." I replied. "I guess I'll just take a couple of weeks off to chill and celebrate another successful long-term job under my belt." I stated.

My principal smiled. "Sounds good." she agreed.

I departed from this position with a feeling of victory. Remote learning was rough for me in the beginning, but I felt that I was becoming acclimated to the new technology and the revolutionary format of learning. My principal's words once again rang tried and true: "The best way to develop an educator's skills is just to throw them in head first and let them figure it out." Baptism by fire was certainly something I was growing accustomed to at this point, and I knew that my next long-term position which was directly over the horizon would be no exception.

Roomers and Zoomers

(February 2021 – March 2021)

The phrase 'roomers and Zoomers' sounds cute and adorable on the surface, but the reality can be quite contrary. 'Roomers' attended class in-person with a teacher, while 'Zoomers' watched live instruction remotely from their homes. The new Hybrid 2.0 model meant acclimating to the new Logitech cameras that had just been installed in every classroom. Not only would all the students in my classroom be vying for my attention, but I would have students who were logged in from home expecting me to respond to their beck and call as well. Of course, my favorite part would be the curious parents peering into my classroom on a daily basis and keenly observing every move I made. I am not sure which I was more elated about: the additional ten pounds that the camera would add to my face and midsection, or the aerobic exercise I would receive from having to constantly shuffle back and forth between my computer and the students in front of me. I was given an opportunity to embark on this new adventure in another long-term position.

Roughly two weeks after my third-grade position ended, I was in the building one day completing a short-term substituting assignment in first grade. My principal asked if she could see me at the end of the day. After I had dismissed my first-graders and thoroughly washed and sanitized my hands, I strolled down to her office.

"Hey," she greeted me. "So, I have some good news… I'm going to need you as a long-term in fifth grade." she explained.

"Oh, awesome!" I replied.

"So, you're going to be in our fifth-grade inclusion room. It'll be a co-teach." Since each grade level team only has one co-teach, I knew precisely which classroom she was referring to. She continued, "Just to give you a heads-up, there are several students in that class with high needs. You also have a friend in a B setting." A B setting in a student's IEP means that they require more intense services that prevent them from being able to participate in the general education curriculum alongside their non-disabled peers at least eighty percent of the time.

I smiled and replied, "Well, you know I'm up for the challenge."

"I know you are." she agreed. "You can feel free to arrange a day or two of transition with that team before that teacher goes out on FMLA."

"I will, and thanks!" I said excitedly.

I arranged a day of transition with the two teachers in the middle of February of 2021. When I stepped into the room, the teacher going out on leave introduced me to the class. "This gentleman is going to be your teacher for the next month and a half. I am going to be gone for a few weeks to handle some things, but he'll take good care of you." she informed them.

The students' spirits were lowered, and I could hear moaning and groaning throughout the room. Since I was familiar with many of these faces from substituting in the building, I said to them, "C'mon, guys, y'all know me. I'm not so bad." I consoled them.

That afternoon, I met with both teachers while the students had their related arts. "So, we split up subjects. I lead language arts and social studies, and she leads math and science," the teacher on impending leave explained. "Now, the marking period ends in a few days, but I'll have all my grades squared away, so you won't have to worry about that." she said, smiling.

"Wow, thank you!" I exclaimed with gratitude.

"Also, you're only going to be responsible for ELA while you're here. I just finished our social studies unit, and my partner will go ahead and teach the next science unit while I'm out. That way, when I come back, I can just pick right back up with the next social studies unit." she added.

"Whoa! You guys have really thought it all out!" I said, excitedly.

My soon to be co-teacher chimed in, "As far as the ELA goes, I'm willing to lead that for your first week until you get familiar with the group and get a feel for the needs and routines in here. When you feel ready, you can pick up the ELA. In the meantime, you can just help out with small group support and assist with some of the students' special education needs."

"Oh, that's not fair to you!" I protested. "I couldn't possibly have you do all my work and teach every subject. I'm here to be your partner, not to shove all the stress and responsibility on you."

The woman shook her head and replied, "Please don't look at it that way. I don't see it that way at all. You're not slacking or shirking your responsibilities. Here, we're a team. We help one another, and do what we need to do to make it all about the kids succeeding." she assured me. It was immediately evident to me how invested both of these women were in their students well-being.

My new placement was located in a classroom at the opposite end of the lengthy hallway where I had spent the last four months. This group of students was far more diverse, and the learning needs in this classroom made those in my previous classroom appear miniscule in contrast. There was one student in particular who was so kind as to ensure that I never endured a single dull moment throughout my school day.

This young man was one of the most unique individuals I have ever crossed paths with. Shortly after getting to know him, I quickly began to grieve the absence of The Wizard and Sergeant Schultz in my life. He had a distinct obsession with the infamous film character *Godzilla* from the 1950s and 1960s. This was the only topic which intrigued him, and it was all he could think about and perseverated on. His random outbursts throughout the day would always pertain to Godzilla.

I was teaching a poetry unit in language arts, and there was a particular lesson at the end of February in which the central focus was on a poem where the narrator compared himself to Godzilla. Surely, he fully engaged in this lesson to such a high degree, that it was nearly impossible for me to concentrate over him. "Godzilla's the man! She will bring destruction! No man can face her!" my impulsive friend shouted.

"All right, Godzilla's the man, we got it. Please be quiet now," I reminded him politely.

However, he carried on, "Godzilla will dominate! She's going to rip all of you to shreds!" he shouted, pointing his index finger around the room at each of his classmates. Thankfully, the rest of his peers had learned not to devote any of their attention to him by this point, much to my relief. They simply ignored his commentary and proceeded as though he was not even in the room.

This Godzilla fanatic shared many characteristics in common with his ultimate hero. Had I so desired, I could have composed my own poem comparing him to Godzilla. One unique quality they shared was their ability to cause chaos and disarray, inflicting misery on anyone in their path.

This young man had a one-on-one paraprofessional who was assigned to work with him. She worked closely with this student, and she suffered verbal abuse from him on a daily basis. His loud screams and chants toward this poor woman still haunt my memory. A particular instance at the beginning of March stands out to me.

As we were wrapping up the poetry unit, one of the last lessons had a writing task that required students to compose their own original poem. Writing tasks were not something this young Godzilla fanatic was fond of. Shortly into the assignment, the quiet ambiance in the room was shaken by "Rrrrraaaaaaaaaaaaa!" All of my students jumped in their seats, and I jolted my head back in shock. "This… is so… hard! I can't do this!" he hollered at the top of his lungs, slamming his hands into his desk!

The para whispered gently to him, "It's okay, just take a deep breath. We'll work through it together, I'll help—"

"Leave me alone!" he screamed, cutting her off mid-sentence. "Why are you always in my face? I've had it with you! I hate you!"

"Sir, you need to calm down." she asserted gently, but firmly.

"No! Why are you so mean? You're so mean to me! All the time! I'm done with you and your mean face!" he shouted.

The young ball of fury chucked his pencil on the floor, jumped out of his seat, and bolted out the door and down the hallway. His brave aide rushed out behind him as he eloped, and chased him as he continued to run screaming down the hallway. About twenty minutes later once she had apprehended him, he came trotting back into the room and collapsed onto the floor. His aide followed slowly behind him, panting and her tongue hanging out from the ordeal. She looked at me, sighed, and just shook her head.

I approached her and whispered in her left ear, "I don't know how you handle this day in and day out." She just sighed again and giggled.

"I'll tell you what," I continued, "if that were me, my friend Tito would be comin' on down off his liquor shelf more often."

"I've just decided to love him and accept him for who he is," she replied. "I just come in with a positive attitude every day, a smile on my face, and a sturdy pair of running sneakers on my feet so I can keep up with this kid." she remarked.

"The Nike company is probably indebted to him for you having to constantly invest in them," I joked.

Remote learning days were far simpler when it came to contending with this furious little firecracker. There was one foolproof solution for rants on Zoom: the magnificent mute button! I employed this strategically throughout numerous Godzilla outbursts. There was one instance in the beginning of March that was particularly memorable.

One day, I was working in a breakout room with a small group where this young gentleman happened to also be. I was reading a poem with my students and explaining the difference between contrast and comparison. "So, guys look at the two stanzas," I instructed. "To compare them, you're pointing out the similarities between them, and to contrast them, you're pointing out the differences—" I was cut off.

"This is too hard, you're so mean! You suck! I'm gonna sic Godzilla on you! She's going to stomp on your face, knock your teeth out, smash you and destroy you!" I reached for my keyboard and simply hit the mute button on Zoom, cutting him off in the middle of his rant. I must admit that this gave me one of the greatest feelings of satisfaction. While I would frequently grow frustrated with this young man, my co-teacher somehow always kept her cool.

In my life, I have encountered few people outside of my own family with a heart like that of this woman whom I shared a classroom with for six weeks. She was a paragon of love, compassion, and patience which was palpable through all of her interactions with each student who walked through her door.

One morning, a student entered the room visibly upset. Tears streamed down her rosy red cheeks, as she sobbed softly and leaned her head against the door. My co-teacher, approached her and wrapped her arms around the girl. "It's okay, sweetheart." She spoke softly. "Tell me what's wrong." She was quick to listen to the young girl's plight, console her, wrap her loving arms around her, and alleviate her pain. In addition, her steadfast example would prove to be an integral part of my journey to becoming a stronger teacher. The amount of professional growth I experienced during my six weeks with her was nothing short of amazing. Differentiating instruction is a unique challenge when teaching the same content; however, she taught me several ways to achieve this more effectively.

My co-teacher was an expert on this method and was one of the lead special education teachers in our building. She showed me many different ways to adjust the format of student assessments, without actually changing the content or any of the material being covered. I also learned valuable strategies for supporting students with reading comprehension and writing deficits. She would ultimately be the one to help me conquer the 'roomer and Zoomer' challenge at hand.

Whenever I think of the meaning of 'differentiated

instruction,' I just think of how bizarre some of my requests are when I order at a restaurant. One particular restaurant I used to patronize as a child charbroiled all of their burgers. Since I have always detested that revolting charbroil taste, I would ask the server to instruct the kitchen to place a piece of tinfoil under my burger while cooking it. I received many looks of annoyance and amusement for this request. Also, whenever I order any beverage aside from water, I always tell my server, "No ice please! I don't want my drink diluted!" My favorite restaurants have always done their due diligence in accommodating my odd requests. So, I prefer to compare a classroom to a restaurant. My students are almost like patrons. It is my duty to offer them their own personalized learning 'menus' that meet their unique needs, which is what differentiation is really all about.

One of my favorite movement activities to introduce to my students is a game named *Statue Garden*. It is a very popular game among various different age levels. During my time in this position, I introduced this game to my fifth-grade class. I explained the directions to the class.

"Okay, friends. My role in the game is to act as the gardener, and you all are going to be statues." I explained. "The objective for statues is to move and shift positions while the gardener cannot not see them. If they are caught red-handed by the gardener, they are out. Naturally, statues do not make any noise, so if I hear you at all, you're out. And another thing… If I can make you laugh, you're out. And I must warn you, I am *very* skilled in this area and my statues can't resist my foolish antics." I challenged them.

I began counting down. "You have ten seconds – ten, nine, eight… Three, two, one… All right, my statues; I'm coming to get you," I sang. I stalked around the room, maneuvering around to each student. I stood in front of them, making ridiculous jokes. In a southern accent, I began, "A little boy was on a farm with his father, when he spotted these brown objects on the ground. He asked his father, 'Dad, what are these?' The boy's father then replied, 'Son, those are smart pills.' 'Smart pills? So, if I take them, they'll make me smarter?' the little boy asked. 'Oh yeah, they sure will," said the dad. The boy then picked one up and tasted it. He shrieked, 'Yuck dad! These are cow turds!' The boy's father smiled, looked at him, and said, 'See, son, you're getting smarter already!'" Half of my statues roared with laughter at this joke, and were immediately eliminated from the game.

While I was still student teaching, I actually caused a student to vomit on the floor in a fit of laughter. The phone call to the nurse explaining why he was being sent down and the reason he needed a change of clothes definitely ranks within the top one hundred awkward phone calls I have had to make in my lifetime. This game was always a favorite when I taught in-person. The problem was discovering how to adapt this game to virtual learning.

Later on, my co-teacher pulled me aside. "Hey, I just want to give you a heads up that I got an email from one of our virtual parents about your game." she calmly stated. "The parent feels like her child was excluded and didn't have the opportunity to participate. I totally get that some things are harder to do with our virtual kiddos, but we've got to make things equitable." she gently explained.

"Yeah, this is going to be tough to include virtual kids in. But our in-person kids love it so much. I'd hate to take it away from them." I replied.

"Well, I think there is a way you could adapt for the six Zoomers we have," suggested my partner.

"How's that?" I asked, scratching my beard.

"Here's my thought: while you're playing, just periodically stick your face in the Logitech camera and try to make them laugh. You can take my laptop around the room with you and watch them to see if they crack."

"Hmm… That just might work!" I agreed.

As ridiculous as I felt making this adjustment, I put her suggestion to the test. Albeit the experience was not the same for my Zoomers, it still provided a solution nonetheless. I even managed to crack a few statues on Zoom, and one of them doubled over with laughter.

As the end of March rolled around, our school district moved to the next phase of hybrid learning. Wednesdays were still asynchronous; however, 'roomers' would now receive four days of face to face instruction rather than two. This was especially a blessing for one of my students with an IEP for a disability that drastically impacted his skills across all academic areas.

I was working with him in a Zoom breakout room one afternoon on an assignment that involved adding and subtracting decimals. The activity involved word problems with money. I was attempting to help him relate to the concepts by illustrating base ten pieces on zoom. "Okay, so think of each individual unit as one cent," I explained. "So, in our ten-strip piece, how many cents are there?" I could hear an audible background noise of the television, which was drowning out the sound of my voice through the screen for him.

Finally, he replied, "Ten."

"Good!" I said. "So, what would a hundred strip represent?" I asked.

"Huh?" the student asked me, holding his right ear up against his iPad.

"What would a hundred strip represent?" I reiterated louder.

"I'm having a hard time hearing you!" he shouted into the microphone.

I resorted to messaging him in the chat, asking him to please turn down the volume of whatever show was playing in the background. I watched as he stood up from his seat on the blue sofa in his living, and approached a dark-haired, tan skinned teenager whom I assumed to be his older brother. I heard him ask, "Hey, could you please turn that down a little bit?"

His simple, polite request was met with a harsh, "Fuck, dude! Why don't you get the fuck out of my face and shut the fuck up!" My eyes widened, and my jaw dropped open.

I sent another chat message asking the student if he could transition to another room. "No, I can't. My parents don't want me out of this room." he replied. Sadly, some of the students who are in the most desperate need of help do not have the stable home environment to devote their attention to remote learning. I was elated that these individuals would finally be back in an environment conducive to learning four days per week.

During the last Friday of March a few days before spring break, I received a phone call from the substitute coordinator. "Good afternoon!" she cheerfully greeted me. "So, tomorrow is your last day in fifth grade, correct?" she asked.

"Correct," I confirmed.

"I've got some good news for you… I have a middle school principal who is looking for a long-term math sub. I remember you mentioning that you have a math background, so I passed your name on to him. Apparently, he recalls interviewing with you a year or so ago, so he'd like to hire you on for the rest of the year." she explained. I felt a range of emotions at that moment.

"Wow." I replied, then hesitated for a few moments. "I do

love math… And it's good that I have an opportunity for steady work for the rest of the year… But—I-I'm just a little nervous about the age group. I mean, middle school wasn't exactly… well… you know… pleasant for me as a kid. It was kind of traumatic for me. So, of course, I'm feeling a little nervous about this whole ordeal right now." I explained to her.

"I completely understand." she replied empathetically. "But, right now would actually be the perfect time for you to give it a shot. Who knows? You might just fall in love with middle school." she encouraged.

I contemplated for a minute. "I… I guess… I guess I can go ahead and give it a shot." I stammered.

"Awesome!" she boomed. "I'll put you in touch with Dr. S, the principal!"

Dr. S and I scheduled an in-person meeting before the beginning of spring break. We arranged to meet on one of the parent conference days, when students were not present in the building. Meanwhile, I still had two days remaining with my fifth-graders in elementary school.

My final day, as I was seated in my chair that morning, my co-teacher focused the entire class' attention on me. "We have something for you that we created as a class to take with you when you leave us." she told me. She then reached onto her desk, and grabbed a small book. She walked over to me and placed it in my hands. Then, she turned to the class, "Guys, what do we say to him?"

"Thank you for being our teacher while Mrs. K was gone," they recited chorally. I looked down at the book from my partner. It was a scrapbook that she and the students had prepared for me. Every page contained a personalized message from each student in the class.

Without my knowledge, she had taken time to create a Google doc where every student could create a personalized page for me with a message and an image. On my last day, she gathered each student's product together and combined them to form the book. "This was so thoughtful of you!" I exclaimed. "It means so much that you took the time to create something so personal for me." I said to my co-teacher.

To this day, she is still an integral part of my journey as an educator and someone that I look to as a mentor for guidance. I would miss working with her for the remainder of the year as I headed to middle school.

Moved Up, but Not Promoted

(April 2021 – May 2021)

I fondly remember my eighth-grade social studies teacher as a fair and kind, but also a very wise lady. Her favorite saying was, "Middle school students are all on drugs: Estrogen and Testosterone." Truer words were seldom uttered. There were still two months of the school year remaining, and I wanted one more long-term position to finish out the school year. I was somewhat hesitant about accepting a role in middle school. My middle school experience had been tumultuous, and my memories of adolescence were filled with bullying, confusion, social awkwardness, as well as searching for my sense of identity. After conferring with several colleagues and educator family members, I decided to be open minded and give middle school a second chance. *Afterall, it's only for two months*, I rationalized. Therefore, I accepted the challenge. I was headed to sixth grade.

I attended my meet and greet with the principal, Dr. S the Wednesday before break; however, after becoming better acquainted with him, I nicknamed him 'Dr. Shithead.' Dr. Shithead was an oversized cue ball, and he resembled a taller version of Mr. Clean, standing at about six-foot-two or six-foot-three. He had poor people skills and lacked integrity, as I would quickly learn.

As I stepped into his office for the first time, he greeted me, "Good morning." He then stood up from behind his desk and walked over to the large rectangular table in the corner at the front of his office. He pointed to a laptop and an iPad sitting on the table. "These are yours." he said, in a monotone voice. He then sat down at the table and gestured with his hand for me to take a seat as well. "So, let's get right to it. You're going to be in the sixth grade. Here's your schedule." He handed me a yellow sheet of paper torn out of a legal pad. "You have four blocks during the day," he explained. "The first hour of your day is for team meetings, parent phone calls, and planning. You'll also have two fifty minute blocks in the middle of the day for planning." He continued, as he shifted in his seat.

Pointing to a line at the bottom of the yellow sheet in my hand, he stated, "This is the teacher I'm going to have you shadow for your first two days. You can go ahead and send her an email. Our instructional coach will be in touch with you regarding curriculum details. Any questions?" he asked me.

The Friday preceding our meeting, I spotted a permanent posting on the district's employment website for the sixth-grade position I was about to serve in as a substitute. Shithead had promised me an interview, but still had not scheduled a date with me yet, despite the fact that the posting had closed at this point.

"Well, I just want to let you know, sir," I started slowly, "I'm still interested in the full-time position, and I'd love the opportunity to interview with you."

He nodded and then replied, "Don't sweat so much about the interview. I'm not that interested in what I can get out of someone during a thirty-minute conversation. Anyone can be a superstar in an interview, but that tells me nothing about how they perform in that classroom. Your real 'interview' here is going to be how you handle the first few weeks in your assignment. I'm going to hold off for at least another month or several weeks before I fill the position or make any decisions. I want to see you work your magic with those kids." he elaborated. My heart raced with excitement. I felt a strong sense of hope.

"Sounds good! I just have one more question... My certification is in elementary education and in special education up through twelfth grade, but I don't have middle school math certification. That won't be a barrier, will it?" I asked.

"Nope. Not at all." He assured me. It sounded as if he was extending me a golden opportunity to let me reveal my worthiness of a position through demonstrating my skills as an educator, rather than through my interviewing skills. Still being fairly naïve and gullible, I believed that the words from this shithead were genuine. I would soon see his true colors.

The 'roomer' and 'Zoomer' ordeal was very similar at the middle school level. The only difference was the added chaos. Coming from an elementary school where classes had been self-contained and I saw roughly thirty students per day, a bell schedule was quite an adjustment. The day was divided into seven blocks, and I was assigned to teach math during four of those blocks. I was granted planning time during the other three. The rumor that elementary school teachers always receive the shaft when it comes to planning time is no falsehood. I am not in any way implying though, that middle school was a breeze. Having four fifty-five minute classes to manage everyday can be a logistical shitstorm, especially when keeping track of which hormone crazed teenagers you are supposed to be responsible for each day proves to be a near impossible task.

Entering into this assignment, I had zero access to any of the information that I needed. We use a database in my district known as eSchool, for entering grades, documenting disciplinary infractions, looking up student demographic and parent contact information, accessing information about students' special education needs, and for taking attendance. Having my eSchool account transferred over from one school to another should have been a seamless process; yet, I began my new role with nothing, despite the middle school having two weeks prior notice that I would be joining them. I still tried to keep a positive outlook, and decided to harass anyone and everyone I could until I obtained my eSchool access. My first week on the job was filled with about an entire month's worth of adventure.

The first two days, I observed the veteran math teacher on my grade level team who Dr. Shithead instructed me to shadow. This woman had amazing classroom management and a very strong content knowledge. She was always very aware of every student's behavior and whereabouts at every given moment, and students were crystal clear on what her expectations were. She cultivated an environment where students were held to high standards and they took pride in their work. Her lessons were very structured, leaving students with no 'down time' during the block that could allow them opportunities to engage in off-task activities. I felt fortunate to have someone like this helping me get my feet wet before wandering alone into the snake pit.

The first class of the day was my advanced math group. Teaching them during the very first block in the morning was equally rewarding as eating dessert before dinner every single night. My second and third blocks were also a pleasure to teach and interact with. Luckily, many of the students in this middle school recognized me as either their student teacher or long-term substitute in elementary school.

"Why don't you come up to the front of the room and say a few words." The veteran teacher said, as she waved and gestured for me to stand before the class.

I stepped forward slowly, my heart pounding rapidly. "Hey everyone! I'm super excited to be your new math teacher." I managed to utter. I proceeded, "I do see a few familiar faces in here… If you had me in elementary school as either your student teacher or long-term substitute, go ahead and stand up." Roughly one-third of the students in each of my first three classes rose from their seats. "Awesome!" I smiled. "So, a lot of you already know me and I know you, so we're going to have a great time together!" One of the students in the advanced class who recognized me from their fourth-grade school year raised their hand.

"Yes?" I answered.

"Are you going to be with us for the rest of the year? We've already had five math teachers. Are you our last one?" she asked me.

I shrugged. "Honestly, I can't say with one hundred percent certainty that I'll be with you until the end of the year." I replied. "However, I can tell you this much… I've spoken with Dr. S and I told him that I would like to stay on as your permanent teacher. It's a decision that he'll make, so I really can't answer that." She nodded her head.

Already having established a solid rapport with at least a third of the students in my class years ago helped to alleviate much of my anxiety, as was the case with them as well. However, the last block of my day was one of the rudest awakenings in my entire life.

I recall how at the end of my very first day, the in-person block seven students came loudly and profanely storming into the classroom, pushing and shoving one another and kicking the desks as they graced my new colleague and I with their presence. While attempting to get these rambunctious children of the corn settled, we also began to admit our virtual students to our Zoom meeting so they could attempt to participate in what was supposed to be a math class.

Throughout the block, the veteran teacher who I was observing had to continually pause her instruction due to the level of disruptions that took place almost every two or three minutes. Watching a strong, seasoned teacher with decades of experience struggling to get through a full lesson, struck fear into my core. It is probably also worth noting that although there were roughly forty students zooming into her class that day, there were roughly the same number of students in the classroom with us simultaneously. The reason for this was the explanation for how the opening for my long-term substitute position came about. The other full-time sixth grade math teacher in the building had resigned in an untimely fashion, tendering her notice one day prior to her final day of duty. Given that there was a shortage of short-term substitutes willing to venture into a middle school and I needed time to finish out the remaining number of days in my previous position, there was no coverage available for my roster. So, there was only one viable solution. The administration was forced to combine each of my classes with this teacher's classes, until I was fully locked and loaded. I would quickly learn more about what I was stepping into.

Although the last block of my first day shook me, I refused to allow myself to become discouraged so early. I sat down with this teacher and listened as she brought me up to speed. "Just so you know, you're their fifth math teacher this year," she explained.

"Fifth?" I asked, shocked.

"Yep. The other four stepped down this year."

"Well, I made a commitment and I intend to stay as long as

I'm needed, even if that's until the end of the year," I tried assuring her.

"Their last teacher said the exact same thing I'm hearing from you right now. She only lasted a little less than two months. I think block seven played a big part in that," she replied. I felt all of the blood drain from my face, my pulse increased, and a wave of nausea washed over me. The conclusion of the school year had seemed so near when I signed on for this new role. Now suddenly, it seemed like an eternity. *I guess I'm really gonna have to be a tough son of a bitch to survive this hell ride and outlast her,* I thought to myself.

My brief period of shadowing ended after two days. I had one asynchronous day in the middle of the week, when the kids would simply complete independent work on their own time without any live instruction. This would allow me time to transition to being on my own in this role. This was a transition that required both physical and emotional preparation. I reluctantly left the safe confines of my Honda Civic on that Thursday morning, with thoughts that I could still flee now before suffering any of the humiliation that would most likely ensue. Wearing my bright orange polo which was tucked into my khaki pants, I marched into the E-shaped building in my brown loafers. I felt like a giant pumpkin who had just been plucked from its patch. Walking down the lengthy hallways, passing all of the tall blue lockers, trying to locate my wing of the building filled me with the polar opposite of nostalgia. I felt the same awkwardness I felt as a middle school student, passing all of the unfamiliar adolescent faces staring at me, the new stranger on campus. I finally located my classroom and began setting up for my day.

Being that this middle school was much older than my

brand-new state of the art elementary school, the technology was also ancient. It seemed that there were more wires involved to connect my smart board, keyboards, and speakers in this classroom than there were cables suspending the Golden Gate Bridge. Unable to figure out the complex process of hooking up my laptop to the smart board, I frantically flagged down the first teacher who had the misfortune of walking past my classroom.

"Hey! Can you come in here for a sec?" I called to her.

"What can I do for you?" she asked courteously.

"I can't figure out all these wires!" I exclaimed in frustration. "How do I hook my computer up to this stupid smart board?"

"First day?" she asked.

"Um, yup." I replied.

She smiled and nodded. "Our technology is old as dirt, just like this school. Here… let me show you," she offered, as she came behind my desk. She clicked a few cords together and, just like magic, everything was up and running. She also got my Logitech camera for my 'Zoomers' rolling.

"Thank you so much! You're my hero this morning!" I said, expressing my gratitude.

"Absolutely! Best of luck!" she replied, as she exited my room and strolled down the hallway. All I had to do now, was survive my first day alone with my teenaged friends.

My first block of the day was my favorite. My advanced group was very grateful to have someone like me, who shared their enthusiasm for math. I began my day feeling relaxed and comfortable, and could run my class in a laid-back manner. My 'Zoomers' in this group communicated with me and made themselves visible and audible. It was the most pleasant eleven twelfths of an hour of my day. Interestingly, there appeared to be no scholastic differences between the 'roomers' and the

'Zoomers' in my advanced block. Both the 'roomers' and 'Zoomers' seemed to be focused, grounded, and driven. Work completion was never an issue among the remote students in my advanced block. They performed equally well, if not better than, their fellow classmates who attended in person. This clearly demonstrated to me that gifted students and those who are academically driven are far more equipped to handle virtual learning. Working in a remote environment does not negatively impact them, and they will still continue to thrive regardless of the fact that they are at home, surrounded by potential distractions. My block one students were a prime example of this.

My second block was also pleasant as well. I always adore a group of students who can appreciate my sarcastic sense of humor. In this group, I only had about twelve 'roomers.' The rest of my block two students were 'Zoomers'. I never saw nor heard from a single one of my 'Zoomers' in this group. Several of them either logged on late, or logged off early. This was status quo throughout my tenure in this position. There was also a dramatic difference between the grades earned by my 'roomers' and 'Zoomers' in this block as well. While all my 'roomers' were excelling and earning As and Bs, almost every virtual student in this block was on the brink of flunking. Clearly, these students were poor candidates for virtual learning. What frustrated me most was that since they were online, they could easily elude accountability and they knew it. The fifty-five-minute block elapsed quickly, leaving me little time to hone in on the 'Zoomers' who were not engaging. Given the fast-pace at which I was expected to implement the math curriculum and the fact that I worked with nearly one hundred and fifty students per day, contacting each parent before a student fell significantly behind was nearly impossible. There was no protocol or process for making a recommendation to shift individuals who were unsuitable for virtual learning to in-person learning. Plus, due to the already more full than ideal classrooms during a pandemic era, additional butt space to offer more students was scarce. I was powerless to change the reality at hand, so I had no choice other than to simply accept it for what it was. After my second block, I had a nice two hour break to divide each half of my day.

My third block of the day after my lunch and planning period was generally peaceful; however, this group struggled immensely with math. Bearing in mind that these students had not had a normal school year since they were in fourth grade, there were a high number of learning gaps. Many of these sixth graders had not been exposed to the critical foundational algebra skills that were a prerequisite to understanding the content I was required to teach. During my student teaching experience, my mentor believed in a skyscraper analogy. Each grade of school for a child is comparable to one story of a sky scraper. It is vital to completely finish building one hundred percent of each level of the skyscraper in its entirety. If construction of each level is less than one hundred percent complete, eventually the skyscraper collapses. I believe that this is what I was witnessing with this particular group of students. Fortunately, I was able to help bridge some of those gaps.

One of the major gaps impeding this group of sixth graders was that they lacked basic understanding of what a fraction was. The majority of the students in this block did not realize that the denominator of a fraction represents the number of equal pieces a whole is being divided into. When I taught students in fourth grade, I always told my students, "Guys, it's all fun and games until you start adding and subtracting denominators." These adolescents made this error at least once on every checkpoint or quiz. I was forced to bring out my visual model for fractions, to show them *why* when they add and subtract fractions, the size of the pieces does not change, which therefore means that the denominator does not change. I also made them take the pledge to be *mathematicians* instead of *mathmagicians,* and stop attempting to perform magic math by adding or subtracting denominators. However, having a group of students who struggle academically is far more desirable than a group who has forgotten how to behave in a normal classroom setting.

My last block of the day was pure hell. The moment they entered my room, I felt like I was starring in my very own remake of *Stand and Deliver.* I was overtaken by a strong feeling of empathy for Jaime Escalante when he stepped foot in his inner-city Los Angeles high school for the first time. As these students entered my room, my ears were flooded with riotous laughter, obscene vulgarities, racial slurs, and derogatory comments. Desks were toppled over onto the floor, iPads were thrown, pencils flew in every direction, and every type of fidget toy ever invented seemed to come flying out of the woodwork. It took me several minutes of playing whac-a-mole with my 'roomers,' before I was finally able to make it over to my laptop to admit my 'Zoomers' into class. Taking attendance was nearly impossible. The noise level inside my room prevented me from being able to hear a single response from any of my students on Zoom. I was forced to switch my Zoom audio from my Logitech camera to my laptop, which I had to hold an inch from my ear in order to comprehend a single utterance from my 'Zoomers.'

For one brief moment, I was forced to turn my face in the opposite direction of my students in order to try to focus on submitting my attendance roster. This was a mistake I would come to regret. I was stunned by a stray bouncy ball which struck me in the forehead, nearly causing me to drop my school issued laptop on the floor. As I attempted to teach the lesson, I was constantly interrupted. By the end of the class period, I had still not managed to be able to cover two-thirds of the content which I had finished with my other three blocks. My 'Zoomers' did not have a single clue about anything I had attempted to teach the last fifty-five minutes. My voice was drowned out by the chaos that ensued, making it impossible for a single word I spoke to be audible to my virtual students. By the time class had ended, I had been forced to neglect more than fifty student chat messages on Zoom, due to my need to have my feet constantly glued to roller skates. I realized that my students on Zoom had suffered immensely from all the disruptions and had essentially retained none of the information. I knew that these virtual students were equally frustrated by the shituation as I was. I also had no doubt that many parents working from home most likely had taken notice of the atmosphere in my classroom as well. Although I had merely inherited this mess and was not even afforded a short honeymoon period, I was determined to salvage the shituation and at the very least, ensure my 'Zoomers' could hear one complete sentence when I spoke.

The first two days, I felt completely powerless during my final block of the day. At the end of the block, there was a twenty minute flex time period where students were encouraged to seek out a teacher in any particular content area where they needed additional help. Of course, my last block of the day was the group that stayed in my room during flex time. By the time this flex block rolled around, I was far too exhausted to even stand on my feet. I collapsed in my chair and gasped for a breath of air. At that point, I had done my best to teach my math lesson to that class but I no longer had the energy to fight the good fight. Trying to control them during those last twenty minutes leading up to dismissal was not a mountain I was willing to die on. Resolved not to end my day in tears on a regular basis, I began to devise a plan.

There were three particular students in this class who were the primary source of my daily migraines. I quickly identified them as the main catalysts of all the disruptions in my classroom. The first two, who I called my 'high flier girls' were extremely defiant to a degree which I was not accustomed to. As someone with an elementary school background, my biggest battles with students were generally chattiness and simple off-task behaviors. Suddenly, two girls rivaling me in size were staring me straight in the face and brazenly refusing to follow a single one of my directions, let alone even so much as pretend to tune in while I was teaching. To the third student, who was my biggest obstacle, I awarded a nickname. A wannabe rap artist who considered himself an 'original gangsta' as he so eloquently put it, saw no need to value his learning nor the learning of others. I remember how he constantly listened to smut music in class, shouted the 'n' word and the 'f' word across my classroom, threw pencils and hit everyone he felt like and mocked me non-stop. Therefore, I dubbed him 'Jammin' Jackass'.

One of the two young girls in my last block seated herself in the back of my room. Her hood was pulled over her head, her cell phone was visible, and she was having an extremely inappropriate sidebar conversation. I overheard her saying to a classmate sitting next to her, "Fuck, girl! Look at these bitches right here! They be bussin' with this shit!" I was unable to make any grammatical or logical sense of this dialogue.

I approached the girl and politely asked her, "I need you to please move up front with me." She simply stared at me, exchanged a look with the other student sitting next to her, and then laughed in my face. "I don't think you're making a great choice right now." I said to her.

"Oh? You don't think I'm making a good choice?" she mocked. "You think you my daddy or something?"

The bystanders began snickering and uttering, "That's right, girl."

"No, I'm your teacher." I replied. "And I need you to pull your hood down, kindly tuck your device into your pocket, and move up front like I've asked so politely." She rolled her eyes and let out a long groan, before finally getting up and stomping up to the front of the room. Five minutes later, she decided to get up out of her seat and slip out of my classroom without permission.

The second high flier girl was actually quite intelligent and full of potential, but preferred to show off for her classmates. Every two or three minutes, I would hear a giant thud and would turn around to see her laughing hysterically.

"Oh, I'm sorry, ma'am—oops—I mean, uh, sir." Her iPad battery was conveniently dead, and she would of course tell me, "Oh, dude, I'm so, so sorry. I can't do any work today." As I would be in the middle of teaching, she would abruptly shout out random disruptive comments. As I was showing students how to cross multiply for solving percentage problems, she hollered, "Yeah; that's the percent of the time I can stay awake in this class," causing everyone to crack up. However, her disruptions paled in comparison to Jammin' Jackass, who prevented his classmates from learning the most.

Unfortunately, Jammin' Jackass never knew the meaning of a stable home environment. A product of a single working mother who placed little emphasis on the value of education, he essentially had one major strike against him to begin with. I never even received a single response to the multiple methods of communication that I used to reach out to his mother.

He came storming into my room on the first day, singing at the top of his lungs, "Yo! I'm in the mother fuckin' house bitches!" His ripped black jeans were sagging to reveal his unsightly plaid boxers. He wore a cheap pair of dollar store sunglasses, and a rugged hat covered his head. He pulled out his phone and began to blast *My Neck, My Back,* an original rap song by the one and only Khia. The lyrics echoed throughout the room, and the phrase 'all you ladies pop your pussy like this' flooded my ears.

"Turn that noise pollution off!" I demanded.

"Yo, man! Chillax!" replied Jammin' Jackass. "This is some good shit right here!"

"Yeah, maybe if you're tone deaf." I mumbled under my breath.

"I don't need none of this math, I'm gonna be a professional when I get out of school, dog." he claimed. I just smiled and continued attempting to instruct the class.

Shortly afterward, I was circulating around the room to assist students with some practice problems when I saw Jammin' Jackass chuck a pencil at another student, striking another student in the forehead. "Fuck you, you dumb ass!" he hollered, raising his middle finger on both hands. I called the front office and asked for someone to come and remove him from the room. This was the first discipline referral that I'd had to write all year.

Fortunately for my other two challenges, their parents were very invested in their educational success. The mother of my second flier girl was appalled to hear about her daughter's classroom antics. The moment she answered the phone and I greeted her, I heard a familiar voice in the background groaning, "Oh my God!"

"I just wanted to let you know that I'm concerned with how your daughter has been behaving in my block." I explained. "She comes in without her iPad charged, she is disruptive, and won't get any of her work done. I've tried switching her seat, but she still looks for ways to engage inappropriately with other classmates who I try to separate her from."

"Really?" the mother asked, shocked. "Well, I'm mortified to receive a phone call like this. This is not how I raised her, and she knows better than to act like this in class. She knows I don't tolerate any kind of disrespect. You *will* see a change in her behavior right away. And if you have to call me again, I'll be reaching out to Dr. S and arranging to come into the building and sit in each of her classes with her." I immediately noticed a total one-eighty in her attitude and behavior. As everyone is probably well aware, having your mom attend your class with you is not what every 'bad-ass' teenager dreams of.

My phone conversation with the other girl's mother was quite disheartening. I will never forget the emotional reaction of this woman. I began the call by explaining to her my reason for calling, and provided her with examples of her daughter's comments and actions. I will never forget the next words from her mouth. "I'm at my wit's end!" she cried. "I've tried literally everything, and nothing gets through to her. I'm fed up, and I honestly don't know what else to do. I'm actually thinking about sending her to a special school at this point, because I really don't think there's anything else I can do for her at home." There was a long pause in the conversation. She was straightforward, and bluntly told me, "Look, I'm going to address this with her, and I'm going to do everything in my power to try and correct this.

But, I just want you to know, I sadly can't sit here and give you a guarantee that you're going to see any change in my girl's behavior. I really can't promise you anything." This shined a light on a grotesque reality.

When a student's behavior becomes too erratic, few options exist for parents or the public-school system. If schools are unable to meet a student's educational needs, they are forced to provide an alternative setting for the student. Naturally, the burden of financing these costs falls upon the already thin-stretched budgets of districts, which in turn leads to a domino effect of having to sometimes deprive other students of necessary resources. Administrators may even find themselves in the unenvied position of having to decide between hiring an additional behavior support aide for a disruptive student or another teacher to help regulate already soaring class sizes. Then, there are parents, like this particular one, who want to support their child's teachers and help correct the problems but have no external support accessible to them. When a parent struggles with their child's outrageous behavior and has exhausted nearly every potential solution, drastic alternatives exist few and far between. There are few options, if any, short of sending a child to a short-term boot camp or military school when a parent no longer feels that he or she has the ability to reach their child. This particular parent was a single mother of three children, working day and night to provide for them. While I was able to form a solid partnership with this woman, there were only so many lengths to which she could climb to constantly maintain control of every detail pertaining to her daughter's education. In addition to both schools' and parents' hands being bound in numerous situations, there is also a progressive discipline philosophy rapidly creeping its way into many schools. My middle school was one example.

'Restorative practices' is a new fad that has been ringing through many hallways. This philosophy was not one I had previously been acquainted with prior to accepting this position. The teacher who I shadowed explained the concept to me in detail.

"So, basically we're not supposed to use real consequences any more." she explained. "The idea of 'restorative practices' is to replace consequences with methods that teach conflict resolution and self-reflection. Basically, all we can do now is pretty much just talk to students and have conversations about what they did, why it was wrong, and what they can do differently. But, the whole idea of restorative practices is to completely avoid taking a student out of the classroom for any period of time." I just rolled my eyes.

"That all sounds great on paper, but there's absolutely no logic behind it!" I vehemently protested. "I mean, how can we not have a backup plan when these so called 'restorative practices' don't get through to those few out of the box kids? It's almost like telling our military that they should only use 'restorative practices' when we have an enemy trying to attack us. Should we just have them eradicate the use of traditional weapons and rely only on conflict resolution to protect our national security? That's basically how ridiculous this restorative practice bullshit is!"

"Oh, I agree with you one hundred percent," she replied. "But unfortunately, that's the future of our school. Dr. S really backs restorative practices, and he's been pushing it ever since he took over here." *Ha! No surprise there,* I thought.

Fortunately, there actually was a drastic de-escalation after this phone conversation with that single parent. I felt that still, one additional step in my plan was required. I decided to use my resources within this new school.

After two days of living in hell during my last hour of the day, I decided to approach my principal, Dr. Shithead. He was sitting behind his desk, his eyes fixed on his computer monitor and his hands were plugging away at his keyboard. I knocked on his open door. "Yes?" he mumbled.

"Do you have a moment? I'm not disturbing you, am I?" I asked.

"You kind of are, but you're already here so just come in," he hissed, not even glancing up from his monitor. I stood awkwardly before him.

"So, the reason I'm here is because I want to talk to you about my last block of the day. You see, it's only been two days and I'm seeing some very radical behaviors. I was hoping we could maybe chat about a possible solution for some of the behavioral problems in this block. I had an idea, and I'd be willing to do all the work and I'm willing to put in the extra time to carry it out. I'd just need your permission. My thought was—"

"You're in the wrong office," he abruptly cut me off. "We have an assistant principal and two interventionists in our building. You have a discipline problem, take it up with them," he dismissed me. "Now, if you'll excuse me, I need to finish this email," he said, as waved his right hand toward me, shooing me out the door, still refusing to make any eye contact with me.

I approached the assistant principal and arranged a meeting with him the very next morning. This gentleman was a realist, much like me, and he proved to be my greatest supporter throughout my tenure in this position.

"Good morning!" he greeted me with a warm smile. "So, I understand you're having some issues in your last block?" he asked.

"Yes, several." I told him. "I've never experienced such a level of defiance before. I almost feel like I have no authority in my own room. They won't even sit in their assigned seats when I ask them to. I have one student who swears the entire period, blasts rap music and sings the vulgar lyrics out loud, calls his classmates highly offensive names, puts his hands on whoever he feels like, and throws shit across my room." He sat listening and nodding.

"So, I have a possible solution, but I want to run it by you first... I was thinking about maybe keeping my three highest fliers after school. If they have to be accountable and stay on their own time to make up the work that they don't do in class, maybe they'll start pulling their acts together." I suggested. Leaning back in his chair, he thought for a moment, took a deep breath, and then began to speak.

"So, I appreciate that you're willing to do whatever it takes to make the situation better and provide a safer environment for your students," he started. "But here's my issue with that idea: the last thing I want to see you do is punish yourself. Why should you have to suffer and give up your personal time when they're goofing off in class?"

I nodded in agreement. "I see your point."

"Plus, it's a liability issue, you know as well as I do one of those kids might retaliate and make up a bogus allegation." He added.

"True," I replied. I couldn't deny this man's logic.

"Here's what I think we should maybe try instead," he proceeded. "We're currently using the library as an overflow lot for social distancing purposes when class sizes are too large. So, I'm thinking one thing we can try here, is having you create a rotating schedule where you send a few students down to the library each day. They can zoom in to your class from there. Just be sure you don't send the exact same students every day." This was a strategic solution that would naturally eradicate some of the behavioral problems, without singling them out for disciplinary action, nor would it result in any loss of instructional time.

"There's also one more step I want to try. Our two interventionists and myself are going to take turns periodically popping into that last block. We're going to make sure though that our presence doesn't undermine your authority. When we're there, we'll just be in the background supporting. It's important for the students to see you as the person who's ultimately in charge of the classroom." he elaborated. "Oh, I think it might also be a good idea for you to touch base with our instructional coach and see if she can offer some more insights." He suggested. I was already feeling relief and hope.

"Thank you so much for all your help!" I cheered. "I'm trying so hard with this block. I know it really sucks for my 'Zoomers' right now, because with all the disruptions they probably can't hear a single word I'm saying in class. I want to turn this classroom atmosphere around, but I have to be honest; it won't be fixed by the next time you walk into my room," I warned him.

He leaned forward in his seat, and said to me, "Listen... You need to understand, Rome was not built in a day. Change will take time. It will take work. Just focus on the progress that you make each day with them. That's what it's all about." He truly understood what it was like to be a classroom teacher and never lost his ability to empathize with other teachers when he was promoted to the office.

I sought the guidance of the instructional coach, as per my

vice-principal's suggestion. The instructional coach welcomed me into her office. "I think some community building and relationship building activities would be perfect for your last block." she claimed. "There are lots of activities you can use that will work with both your 'roomers' and 'Zoomers' at the same time. One of these activities is *Two Truths and a Lie*. Are you familiar with it?" she asked.

"Vaguely," I replied.

"Okay, so here's how it works," she continued. "Everyone has to share two statements about themselves that are true and one that's false. Everyone else's job is to guess which of the three statements is false. You should go first to model it." Initially, I was quite skeptical that the activity would yield any positive change.

"Um… Do you really think this going to work?" I asked her. "I mean—they don't take anything seriously, and I can barely get through a full minute without being interrupted. I feel like they won't even bother with this game." I said.

"It'll have more of an impact than you realize," she rebutted. "I get that they're teenagers, and that a lot of them think that it's uncool to show feelings or care about school. But I'm telling you, little things like this build a sense of community and make the students feel closer to each other and you." As silly as it may seem, this activity yielded positive results toward helping me develop relationships with this challenging group of students. *Two Truths and a Lie* inspired a number of inquiries about my personal life among these adolescents.

I began my with my three statements. "All right, guys… I'm going to share three statements with you about myself. You've got to figure out which one is a lie. I drive a Honda Civic. I love to watch football. I live in another state."

The students turned to each other, and I could hear them whispering and speculating. Jammin' Jackass was the first to call out, "Well, the first one ain't the lie, 'cause I saw you get out of that piece of shit when I got off the bus this morning!" The entire block roared with laughter. I just smiled, and decided to save face in front of my class.

"You're right, it's definitely not the fanciest. When you make it as a famous rap artist and you've got your own record label, you'll be able to buy a much nicer one." I retorted sarcastically. My class once again burst out into riotous laughter.

Of my two higher flier girls one stood up and said, "I'm going to have to go with the second one as your lie, because I can see you're too dorky to watch sports."

"The second one *was* my lie! You got it!" I exclaimed. "But, even though I'm not into sports, I actually am a WWE fan." I shared.

"Have you been in person?" asked Jammin' Jackass.

"As a matter fact, I have!" I proudly proclaimed. "My dad, my step brother, and I went a couple years ago in my grandpa's memory. We were up in the front row. I even flipped off the Miz and his merry band of morons, the Miztourage."

I heard gasping throughout the room. "You actually flipped someone off?" one of my students asked in disbelief.

"Yup! Sure did! I gave 'em all the bird on both hands." I smiled.

The inquiries began coming forth. "Have you wrestled anyone before yourself?"

"Have you ever beaten anyone up?"

"Have you ever actually played a sport in your entire life?"

I replied, "You know, I like to leave the action up to athletes."

"How old are you?" one of them asked me.

"Older than you, but below thirty," I replied.

"Are you married?" another student asked me.

"No," I responded.

"Who do you live with?" one of my two high flier girls asked.

"Okay guys, I think we're getting just a *little* too personal here. I think you've learned enough about me for now. Let's move it on to you all." I said, as I passed it on to each of them.

I found my instructional coach later that day. "Phew! I tried *Two Truths and a Lie* with my last block, and boy was that awkward!" I vented.

"Why is that?" she asked puzzled.

"They asked me all these weird personal questions, like how old I was and if I was married." I explained.

My instructional coach then smiled and pointed out to me, "That's actually a great sign. They're interested in you, and they care enough to ask you these questions and get to know you better." It then occurred to me that her insight was accurate, and that perhaps, I was finally managing to break the ice. This woman also took the time to observe my class both in-person and from Zoom in order to gain a perspective from both lenses. She was able to provide me with valuable feedback and offered me with what were seemingly simple logistical suggestions to ensure my 'Zoomers' were having better access to learning. Some of these suggestions made a significant impact, much to my surprise.

"I would suggest making use of emphatic statements." she offered.

"Emphatic statements?" I asked, clueless. "What's an 'emphatic statement'?"

"So, basically an emphatic statement is when you let others

know how you feel about something they're saying or doing by inserting yourself into the equation. For example, when you see one of your kids is ready to blow up at you and go on a rant, you can say to them 'I know you're angry with me, and I'm glad you're honest.' Or, you could maybe say, 'I understand how you feel and your feelings are not wrong.' If you have a student that starts going off on you and raises their voice, you can say to them 'it makes me feel disrespected when you talk to me that way'."

I was very skeptical of this suggestion. "I'm afraid that might just provoke them and make things worse." I rebutted.

"It really won't. You're always going to have those one or two that don't respond to just about anything, but I think you'll find that it works for the most part." she assured me.

Initially, although I was discreet about my opinion in the presence of my instructional coach, I was thinking to myself that this emphatic statement idea was ridiculous and would bear no fruit in solving any of problems. Trying to keep an open mind, I decided to attempt it anyway. The results I observed in a brief window of time were astounding. These statements actually had a far-reaching impact, and they helped me to successfully deescalate several potential shituations in my classroom.

One day, I had to return an assignment to Jammin' Jackass, which he performed poorly on. "I fucking hate math!" he screamed. "I don't get this shit! It's so fucking stupid!" Instead of scolding him or calling for one of the interventionists to remove him, I walked slowly to his desk and leaned in close to him.

"I get that you're frustrated. There's nothing wrong with that. But when you yell out those types of things, it makes me feel like you don't respect me." He just looked up at me. I was expecting him to escalate, or perhaps even spit in my face.

Instead, he simply mumbled, "Sorry." And then he put his head down on his desk. My coach's suggestion actually worked, and it saved me a phone call to the front office and the trouble of writing a disciplinary referral.

I realized that the reason why these emphatic statements were so effective, was because they actually allowed me to connect to students on their level. It revealed that I truly cared about them, that I valued their feelings, and that I was more to them than just a teacher who they saw for a fifty-five minute block. It was a tool for relationship building, which any bona fide educator will attest is the cornerstone of strong classroom management. I am now a stronger educator, as the result of opening my mind and accepting the guidance of this wise instructional coach.

In addition to the anxiety that consumed me and the amount of energy that I expended from teaching on roller skates each day, the springtime heat was especially brutal this year. I already had a condition known as hyperhidrosis, where I would sweat profusely, particularly underneath my arms. It certainly did not help that my car's air conditioner required a recharge around this time, and I was forced to drive around in a greenhouse for weeks until I was able to arrange a repair.

Middle school students are very perceptive of details like this, and I was unable to successfully conceal my two sweat soaked underarms each day. I could hear the whispers of the students, especially those during my last block of the day. They exchanged jokes and laughter at my expense. "He must have just been carrying some heavy weights around," they remarked, assuming I was deaf. I ignored these snide comments, refusing to let them get the best of me. I also had to ignore comments from 'Zoomers' that were written in the chatroom as well. The fascinating fact about the Logitech cameras, was that they were powerful enough to highlight this detail too. I felt super embarrassed, but played it cool. I was at least satisfied with the improvements in my work day.

I was no longer leaving the building with splitting headaches after dismissal. I will not boast that my last block of the day ran smoothly henceforth and that the disruptions ceased, because that would be an obnoxious fabrication. However, the support I was receiving from my administrator, my communication with families, and the pearls of wisdom my coach had imparted to me were finally beginning to pay off. By my third week on the job, I was able to make it through a full math lesson with my final block. My 'Zoomers' were able to concentrate and hear me clearly, and I even found responding to their questions and their chats to be a manageable task. My 'roomers' were retaining information and achieving academic growth. I was even able to make an impact on Jammin' Jackass.

When I initially began, his math grade was stagnating in the failing range and he had no conceptual understanding of any sixth-grade math standards. By the end of the four-week period that I was in charge of this classroom, his grade had improved to the high C range, and he no longer felt that solving problems was impossible for him. I knew he would not appreciate me enough in the short run to write me a thank you, bring me flowers, or devise a rap song in my honor, but I still hope one day Jammin' Jackass will look back on his experience with me in a positive light. Hopefully, years from now he will have an epiphany and realize that the sweaty, nerdy long-term sub he had when he was twelve years old cared enough to try and reach him. Perhaps someday when he fulfills his aspirations of becoming a famous rap artist and surpasses the number of record sales of that of

Kayne West and 50 Cent, he may be so kind as to give 'that teacher' a shout out on stage in front of his live audience. Or, he might decide to write some bussin' lyrics about me in one of his top hits. Somehow, I get the feeling that extreme patience will be required on my part to see that come to fruition.

Not only did the students reap benefits from my four-week stay with them, but I also gained more familiarity with different technologies. Classkick, a learning platform for modeling and teaching lesson concepts as well as assessing student work samples, was heavily promoted in this middle school. I was amazed by its many mind-blowing features. Classkick allowed me to monitor the progress and whereabouts of every student simultaneously. I could see precisely which slide each student in my class was on, whether or not they were on the correct slide, and I had live viewing ability to see every number or word that a given student was recording at that moment in time. The annotation tools it offered were amazing. This technological platform eliminated the need for my roomers to summon me to their seats, and it also eradicated the need for my Zoomers to compete with my roomers for attention. Classkick offers two features that students can use to indicate that they need help or feedback. When students were struggling on a slide or encountering difficulty with a particular problem, they could press a yellow hand button which would indicate to me that I needed to assist them. When someone completed a problem and wanted me to check for accuracy or provide them with feedback, they could press a green hand button. I was able to come directly to those students' slides and add notes and written feedback to their work, which would be immediately visible to them. This was a way to ensure both my 'roomers' and my 'Zoomers' received equal access to me. Tools like this are invaluable to students and teachers alike, and they are a star in the zombie apocalypse era. I would later learn of many more awesome features that Classkick had to offer upon transitioning to my next assignment.

Before two full weeks into my position had elapsed, Dr. Shithead appeared in my classroom during my planning one afternoon. "I just wanted to let you know that I've come to a decision regarding the full-time position. In a couple of weeks, you're going to be transitioning to seventh grade. We've selected a candidate, and she'll be taking over in a couple weeks." he explained.

I felt as though I had just been punched in the gut. "Wait, I thought that you weren't going to fill this position for a while. Did I do something wrong? Are you dissatisfied with the way I've handled things in the classroom?" I inquired of him. I could not understand why he was delivering me this news, when it had only been roughly a week and a half since I had stepped foot into this nightmare.

"It's got nothing to do with your performance." he answered.

"If you don't mind me asking, why don't you feel like I was a good candidate for this position?" I asked.

"It's your certification, you're missing the secondary math piece for this job." I was astounded, since I had already inquired early on whether or not my certification would present a potential blockade.

"I thought you said my certification wouldn't be an obstacle." I retorted.

Shifting in his chair and breaking eye contact, he stammered, "W-well… I didn't think—I mean, the certification issue just kind of presented itself in the process." It dawned on me at that very moment, that he clearly had absolutely no intention of hiring me from the moment I walked through his door.

I realized that any further discussion on the subject would not change his mind. Resigned to my fate, I did not question him any further. However, I was concerned about how the news would be received by the students and I wanted them to know who was responsible for the impending change. "If you wouldn't mind, would you be willing to come to each block on my last day and help me make the announcement to the students?" I requested.

"Sure, I can do that." he agreed.

The day came upon me quickly, and the principal held true to his word. His news was not warmly received by the students or their families. My advanced class especially did not display a jubilant reaction to this change. One of the students in my advanced block abruptly interrupted the principal in the middle of his thought, and she bluntly asked him, "How many more teachers are we going to have to go through this year? Is this next one going to actually stay this time?"

The principal looked at her with a vague expression and then began to respond to her inquiry. "Well, based on how confident I am on a scale of one to ten that she'll be with you for the next five weeks until summer break, I'm at about an eight or a nine. With all the other teachers, my confidence level was at about a three or a four. So, I think you're in pretty good hands this time."

Another student in my advanced class, was particularly upset too, especially since he was in my student teaching class as a fourth grader when I was reassigned halfway through to take over another classroom as a long-term substitute. "That's not fair," he protested. "First, you had to leave me in fourth grade and now you have to leave me again!" Even my block two students and block three students were disappointed to hear about my departure. A few students even approached me for a hug on my final day. The rarity of a middle school student hugging one of their teachers is practically unheard of, so I felt pretty special. The students were not the only ones who shared these feelings.

Most parents were far from elated over the fact that their children were about be introduced to their sixth teacher for the current school year, with less than five weeks of school remaining.

I received several emails and phone calls from parents, expressing their discontent over the principal's decision to transfer me. Many of them questioned the rationale behind the changes. One parent in particular, whose daughter I had taught in fourth grade was particularly upset.

I spoke with her on the phone the night of the announcement. "My daughter was really upset when she came home. She told me about the change. I can't believe it! A lot of kids and parents are going to be very unhappy!" she exclaimed.

"I'm honestly not thrilled either." I stated.

"Why is he doing this?" she asked.

"Well, Dr. S came in today and explained his logic and reasoning to each of my four blocks today. He felt as though the new teacher he had hired on a permanent contract would be better off starting in the lowest grade of middle school, since her last decade of teaching experience was at the elementary level." I explained.

"Oh, no! First of all, you were there *first*! That's not fair! These kids have already had five different math teachers so far this year! What's he thinking? Throwing in a new teacher for the last five weeks of school makes zero sense, and it's just going to cause more disruption! Plus, if he wanted to hire a *middle school* teacher, then maybe he should've actually hired someone with more *middle school* experience!" she contended.

I sighed. "Unfortunately, it's above my pay grade." I told her, defeated.

Several parents were not appeased by his reasoning, and shared with me that they intended to reach out to him and express their feelings personally. I strongly doubt that any of them were taken seriously, based on my impression of this gentleman's demeanor and my observations of his interactions with other people. I contemplated discussing my feelings about the reassignment and requesting the opportunity to remain in sixth grade for the last few weeks; however, I realized that such a conversation would not be well received.

Though I did not believe it possible, I even found myself having difficulty parting with my last block of the day where the fruits of my labor had finally begun to manifest. My greatest fear was that once I departed, all of my efforts would unravel and the classroom environment would shift once again in the wrong direction.

Sadly, this fear was quickly confirmed. Roughly one week after I was moved to seventh grade, I received a text from the newly hired teacher that read: *Hey! Can you please go ahead and call me as soon as possible?* Naturally, I was intrigued and concerned for my former sixth-grade students. Therefore, I decided to dial her number.

As soon as she answered, I heard her breathing heavily. The first words out of her mouth were, "Oh my God!"

"What?" I asked out of genuine worry and interest.

"Block seven is falling apart! Everything is going straight to hell! A serious fist fight between four students in our last block broke out this afternoon! It was awful! I didn't even witness who started it or what happened at first, because my attention was completely diverted and my back was turned!" she raved frantically.

"Holy shit!" I exclaimed.

"That's not all, there's more! The disruptive behavior in that block has gotten so far out of control! It's almost impossible for 'Zoomers' to hear a single syllable over all the chaos ensuing in my room! One of the parents from block seven got really frustrated and she recorded the audio and video of students nearly swinging from the ceiling! I can't believe what she did next; she actually emailed a copy to the administration!"

My jaw was beginning to drop. "Whoa!" I replied in awe.

To add to the excitement, the third math block in which no prior behavior problems had manifested themselves, was now in full-blown rebellion mode. "And it's not just block seven any more," she added. "I'm having trouble with that third block too all of a sudden! They just completely ignore my authority now! They won't do any work, they won't sit in their assigned seats, they won't put their phones away – it's unbelievable! I even have two students who keep blasting music the entire time, because they think it's funny to prevent me from teaching! I end up losing half that block just trying to get them to shut up! I have no clue what to do!" she cried desperately. I was devastated to hear that all of this was happening. The long-term substitute pay was meager, and I had not poured my sweat, blood, and tears into that assignment merely for the petty compensation. It was aggravating and disheartening to helplessly watch all of my hard work being dismantled.

"Have you reached out to the instructional coach?" I asked. "Oh yeah, we've had our meetings. The thing is though, when she observes me through Zoom, she wants me to face the Logitech camera so that she can see the whole class and everything that's going on in the room. That's the last thing I'm going to do! Ha! I don't want her seeing this hot mess up in here!" she explained. This comment, I found quite unnerving. Concealing is not correcting, as she would soon discover.

Despite my frustrations, I had to redirect my focus to my new assignment. I was now in seventh grade and I needed to concentrate on doing my best to make the adjustment to yet another new grade level. I naively assumed that the shift from sixth grade to seventh grade would be minor and that minimal differences, if any, would exist between the two age groups. However, I would be astounded to learn how vast of a difference one year makes with teenagers.

My Last Long Term

(May 2021 – June 2021)

It was nice staying busy the entire school year with long term positions, unlike the previous year. Being that this transition to seventh grade was my fourth long term assignment in the same year, I was overtaken with fatigue. Each shift from one long-term position to another is similar to essentially beginning an entirely new school year, over and over again. Having to acclimate to a new grade level, a new curriculum, a new group of students, a new routine, and sometimes even a new building multiple times in the same year can be overwhelming. With four and a half weeks of school remaining and the spring temperatures rising, I wanted to be settling on the beach rather than into another assignment. However, I convinced myself that with such little time left in the year, I could handle one last ride.

I was welcomed by my co-teacher, JR. JR had been flying solo all year in an inclusion classroom that should have been staffed with two teachers. As I entered into her room that first morning in my new assignment, I was warmly greeted with a smile. "It's so nice to have you! I'm really looking forward to working together!" she said excitedly. JR was a seasoned woman with dark brown hair and brown eyes, in her mid-thirties. I felt welcome from that moment.

"I'm excited to work with you." I said to her.

"The pleasure's all mine." she replied. "It's been quite a year.

I've been on my own for the last several months. Our first block has seventy students. It's actually two classes combined. One is an advanced class, and one is a regular group." she explained. I was puzzled as to why she was teaching two classes, with a total of seventy students on her own.

"Why are you teaching by yourself that first block with so many students?" I inquired.

"Well, I wasn't *supposed* to be. Originally, they gave me a co-teacher at the beginning of the year. She worked with me the first few months of school up until she left."

I nodded. "I see."

She then continued, "Actually, I'm in a co-teach classroom. My other three blocks have several students with IEPs in them. The way it was planned out at first, was that my co-teacher was supposed to teach the regular class while I taught the advanced group during that first block of the day. Then, she was supposed to support me and pull small groups during the latter three blocks." I immediately felt empathy for JR.

"So, you've been on your own, doing the job of two teachers for the past several months?" I asked in amazement.

"Honestly, I've been on my own really all year. You see, the person they put in here with me who left—well—she wasn't exactly much help. She was petrified of the math. She was so uncomfortable with the content, that she wouldn't teach a class on her own which is why I ended up teaching all seventy kids by myself in that one block. She wouldn't work with small groups, give them feedback on their work, or help me with any of the grading either because she had absolutely no handle on any of the mathematical material."

I just shook my head. "So what *did* she do while she was in here, enjoying a full teacher's salary?"

"Well," JR continued, "one thing she actually didn't mind doing was going through students' slides on Classkick to make sure they were on-task like they were supposed to be. If they weren't starting their work or if they were goofing off, she'd put a 'where are you' sticker on their slide and try to redirect them."

"Oh, wow. That's such a big help." I remarked sarcastically.

JR laughed and nodded.

"The good news is," I proceeded, "you're not on your own any more. I'm happy to take on the grading for you, and I'd love to work with some groups and help with the teaching aspects."

Her eyes widened and her face lit up. "That would be fantastic!" she shouted, throwing her hands above her head. Being able to feel like a hero provided me with a strong sense of gratification.

JR was wrapping up her last math unit of the year: geometry. Although math has always been my hands-down favorite subject, geometry was the one and only part of math that I detested before I co-taught with JR. Students were learning how to calculate surface area and volume of rectangular and triangular prisms. JR and I decided to divide and conquer. While she led the direct instruction, I went in Classkick and provided immediate feedback to all students on their completed work slides. Also, she addressed all of the questions from the 'roomers' while I communicated with the 'Zoomers.' We divided up the grading. Our teamwork definitely made the virtual dream work. I even learned a number of strategies from JR that removed the sour taste in my mouth about geometry.

Seventh grade was a surprisingly pleasant age level to work with. Plus, my co-teacher had established terrific classroom management as well as a genuine rapport with her crew. One day, JR had to leave early and I was left in charge of her last block of the day. This threw my hyperhidrosis into an all-time overdrive and caused me to sweat like a sinner in church. I expected the students to begin cursing, throwing objects, and leaving the classroom the second JR walked out. Much to my amazement, none of this came to fruition. Instead, they decided to play a game of *Hot Seat* with me as a celebrity guest. I felt like I was in the strangest interview of my life.

Just like my sixth graders had done during *Two Truths and a Lie,* my seventh graders also began asking me a series of awkward personal questions that made me want to blush. "How old are you?" one of them asked me.

Another one wanted to know, "Do you have a girlfriend? How many women have you dated?"

There was even a student who had the nerve to inquire, "How much money do you make doing this? Is it enough for you to live by yourself, or do you still have to live with your parents right now?" I was baffled as to why these teenagers were so curious to know so many intimate details about the quiet stranger who dwelled in the back of the room and merely gave them feedback on their work. However, I would soon no longer be just a silent stranger in this classroom.

As was the case with sixth-grade, there was also one seventh grade advanced math class. The last nine days of school, JR decided that her advanced group should be introduced to the Pythagorean Theorem. She and I agreed that during our first block with the two combined classes, I would take the advanced group to a separate location while she worked with the other group on more surface area practice. I loved the Pythagorean Theorem. It is the simplest math concept ever. All it consisted of was memorizing the formula $a^2 + b^2 = c^2$ and being able to substitute in two sides of a right triangle for two of the variables, and then simply just solving for the missing side.

I watched the faces of my advanced students turn pale as snow when the words 'Pythagorean Theorem' trickled off of my lips. "We can't do this!" one of them protested.

"There's less than two weeks of school left, this isn't fair! We aren't supposed to have to know this until eighth-grade," another one of them argued.

"Yeah, but you're advanced. So, look at it this way: you're getting an advance on something that the rest of your peers don't have to learn until next year," I rebutted.

I was amused to see such an intelligent group of students intimidated by such a simple concept. I quickly put their minds at ease and alleviated their stress level. To add to my enjoyment, I taught Pythagorean Theorem with a new technological trick I had absorbed from JR. I was in awe of this new technique, screen mirroring.

When I began at the middle school, I had been issued both a school laptop and an iPad. My district purchases and issues Dell laptops, which I am comfortable with because Dell is my go-to computer brand. However, there are three things that I have solemnly sworn to avoid in my life: cigarettes, drugs, and Apple products. Apple and I are not compatible, which is why I rarely made use of the iPad I was given prior to co-teaching with JR. However, she introduced me to the beauty of screen mirroring from my iPad, a feature that would allow me to sync whatever I was modeling on my screen to any active Zoom meeting within proximity. Naturally, I was still intimidated until I tried it for the first time.

Once I experimented with screen mirroring, all of my fears and doubts rapidly dissipated. Being the total nerd that I am, it takes very little to inspire that exultant feeling inside of me when I master anything related to technology. Being able to annotate my iPad screen and model problems all while making my work sync to the smart board and our Zoom meeting was, truly, an empowering experience for me. I felt like breaking out into song and singing *I Got The Power* by Snap. When I told JR how this felt like stepping into a whole new world, she simply just shook her head and grinned at me. I applied my newly acquired screen mirroring abilities to each of my Pythagorean Theorem lessons, and my mind was blown by the positive impact that this feature not only made on my students' learning, but also on my brain. It allowed me to juggle much less while accomplishing so much more with my class. Finally, it appeared I was learning to 'work smarter, not harder'. To my satisfaction, the last three days of school not only were far less demanding, but also quite refreshing.

The seventh-grade team decided to organize a karaoke, where both 'roomers' and 'Zoomers' had the ability to participate. The majority of the 'roomers' in my class boldly volunteered to grace their classmates with their divine vocal stylings, and a shockingly high number of 'Zoomers' opted in as well. This event was located in the school's large auditorium. On stage, there was a computer with a dual monitor set up. All of the students participating via Zoom were on these monitors, and a microphone with the volume cranked up to the maximum was placed next to the computer speakers. The song beats and lyrics were also able to be shared over the Zoom meeting. I was impressed with the level of planning that the teachers underwent to ensure that the event was made equally accessible for all students, both in-person as well as virtual. Sadly, I cannot attest that I was as impressed with the quality of the singing that assaulted my ear drums for two consecutive hours.

The students' performances may not have been American Idol worthy, however they were definitely a hilarious source of entertainment. There were two girls from my advanced math group, who kept volunteering for song after song. I applauded for them each time, meanwhile thinking that they ought to just stick with the Pythagorean Theorem. Seventh graders might be undergoing puberty and going through that awkward transformation in their lives, however they were still kids. Many of them actually enjoyed some of the same goofy activities that I used with my elementary school students.

My seventh graders absolutely loved my statue garden game. I must admit though, getting them to crack was tougher. They knew how to withstand my catchiest jokes, and they were pretty good gardeners themselves. When we alternated roles and I was a statue, I was an easy target to eliminate. Meanwhile, JR had a fun scavenger hunt activity for our 'Zoomers'.

Entering into the summer, I felt that I had grown exponentially as an educator over the past year. At the end of every school year, I always feel that I have come so much farther in my journey as an educator. Then, as soon as a new school year begins, I get an instant reality check that shows me that I still have much to learn, and that all the knowledge I had obtained during the previous year was actually minimal. My brain was exhausted from all of the new information it had absorbed from the new virtual reality it had learned to adapt to this year.

I was ready for break, and I needed time to recharge. I was seeking a summer position that kept me sharp and in practice, but that still simultaneously allowed me time for rest and rejuvenation. I had taught regular summer school before; however, I was seeking an opportunity with less liability and fewer hours this summer. As fate would have it, I found just the opportunity I was looking for.

Throughout my tenure at the middle school, I still maintained frequent communication with my elementary school principal. At the beginning of June, we were having a casual conversation when the topic of summer work arose.

"Hey! I know you're running some summer camps. Any chance you might have a spot or two open for me?" I asked.

"Nah. Unfortunately, it looks like right now I probably have more teachers than I have slots to put them in." she replied. I sighed with disappointment, but understood the fairness of offering the work to the internal candidates first. However, a few days later, she followed up with me.

"So, about those summer sessions – looks like I do have a couple of open spots for you, after all." she exclaimed.

"Great!" I said.

"How do you feel about running some hands-on STEM activities?" she asked.

"Well actually, that would probably be really good for me. I'm always saying how science is one of my weaknesses and I need to grow in that area – this could be a chance for me to do that." I elaborated.

She was pleased to hear my response. "Awesome. I'll send you the Google sign-up sheet!"

I received the sheet from her. There were a few options. One of the options was 'Balloon Boat', and another option was 'Stomp Rocket'. These both sounded challenging; however, they also sounded intriguing. I proceeded to type my name in the slots for each of these activities. I would enjoy a few weeks off before my first session during the first week of July. Being that I had worked practically the entire 2020–21 school year with steady, back to back long-term positions with minimal break time, I was actually grateful to have an opportunity to rejuvenate and recharge.

A Taste of Normalcy

(July 2021 – August 2021)

Two months in middle school made me appreciate elementary school in an entirely new light. I missed my young, untainted friends, and it was time for me to return to where I belonged. The elementary principal who I was working for before the middle school opportunity presented itself, decided that she wanted to offer some enrichment opportunities for students since the pandemic had been so restrictive. Her idea was to offer short STEM camp sessions, where the students would be able to participate in hands-on activities and science experiments. Conveniently, she needed teachers to staff each of these camp sessions. Each session lasted one week, and was three days long. I had been somewhat intimidated by STEM activities, and science was my weakest area. This seemed like a safe and appealing opportunity to grow in this area and strengthen my STEM background. So, I volunteered for a few sessions.

These sessions were offered entirely in-person, meaning that I would be temporarily estranged from my new normal. It felt invigorating to finally be able to work with students again in a normal(ish) classroom environment, without having to worry about a Logitech camera following me everywhere I walked, and without having to constantly dance around between my laptop and my live pupils. One primary disadvantage of remote teaching, is the inability to lead old fashioned hands-on projects with my class. Over the course of this summer, I was able to once again experience one of the joys of teaching that lured me into the profession to begin with.

I was placed in charge of leading one STEM unit, which incapsulated three projects that all followed the same structure and sequence. First, I would assemble prototypes of a specific object for students. It would be their job to deconstruct each prototype, and determine what parts were used in its assembly, as well as the quantity. Next, my students would work in small groups to replicate the design and create their own prototypes. The most engaging portion of the sequence was when students would test their products, and reflect on how successful their designs were. Finally, students would be innovators and explore alternative methods and materials for refining their original designs. These activities were very popular with my summer camp classes, and completely altered my attitude toward science.

My first STEM project was a balloon boat. I was provided a kit with cardboard pieces, liquid paraffin wax, straws, a kiddie pool, and of course balloons. Students loved building their balloon boats and sailing them in the kiddie pool filled with water. The groups whose boats went the farthest got to celebrate with a round of statue garden. The other groups became extremely competitive and took the activity personally. I remember overhearing the conversation one student was having with his group, when their boat fell apart in the kiddie pool. "This is the SS failure, a literal shipwreck," he declared. The final project in this unit was the favorite among my students, and it was my personal favorite as well.

The stomp rocket was epic! When I read the assembly and project implementation guidelines, I could not imagine any type of student who would not enjoy stomping on plastic water bottles to launch custom made wooden rockets into the air. Students designed their rocket launchers with pipes and tubes. They were given balsa wood and sand paper to design the actual rockets that would be launched high into the air. It was my idea to bring in a sturdy wooden platform to jump off of when they dropped their full body weight onto the water bottles. This project was a massive success, in respect to both student engagement and students' designs of their prototypes. Most groups were able to launch their rockets thirty to forty feet in the air, almost striking the cafetorium ceiling. I highly doubt our custodians would have appreciated it if we shattered one of the lights, which we came dangerously close to accomplishing. We were just far too busy enjoying ourselves. This project really showed me how much I truly missed many of the irreplaceable benefits of traditional in-personal learning. However, I still held to my convictions that virtual learning could still be very powerful, provided that the teacher possessed the enthusiasm and creativity needed to run a remote classroom.

This taste of normal, face to face learning would be my last for the time being. Behind the scenes throughout the summer, a master plan was underway by my district to appeal to the wishes of families who preferred remote learning to face to face instruction. My school, along with my principal and vice-principal, were at the forefront of this revolutionary plan that would have a far-reaching impact on not only the dynamics of teaching and learning, but on my future as an educator.

As the beginning of the school year rapidly approached, I was still in search of permanent position. Being that it was now August, I was tripling the efforts of my search, hoping to secure a position soon. As it would turn out, my school had been the place to look all along.

My Big Interview

(August 2021)

Addressing the numerous inadequacies and shortcomings of the 'roomer' and 'Zoomer' model required innovative thinking. The explosive population growth in my district along with families' surging interest in a remote learning platform, demanded an authentic solution. Months of brainstorming finally yielded a collaborative development. The creation of a virtual academy was expeditiously underway, to be hosted by none other than my school.

The virtual academy would completely eliminate the chaotic dubstep teachers were being forced to perform, and it would provide equity for students. Each virtual student would have access to their own teacher, rather than competing with their classmates who were attending in-person learning. Among the factors considered when selecting my school for this great experiment, included its grandiose structure, state-of-the-art technology, amazing administration team, and of course its geek squad. Our building wide instructional technology coach, who was also my mentor during my student teaching semester, seemed to have a divine gift with technology. His heroic mission would entail helping our virtual academy fulfill its purpose of ensuring equitable learning experiences for our remote students. The next step was selecting valorous teachers to staff the virtual academy.

The first round of interviews was offered to internal applicants, whom to the astonishment of few, were in short supply. This meant an opportunity for external candidates, like myself. From the years of devotion and hard work I had sown, I would finally reap the golden opportunity that I had long desired.

I submitted my formal application for one of the virtual academy spots. My principal, being a very transparent lady, leveled with me the moment I expressed interest in a phone conversation. "I'll be frank with you," she began. "I have a lot of reservations about these virtual positions to begin with. These aren't going to be a cake walk, no matter who we end up selecting. Also, you're a novice teacher. The last thing I want to do is toss you into a position where I set you up for failure." She then proceeded to inquire, "Is teaching from a remote learning platform something you're even interested in? How would that prospect make you feel?"

I believe in being positive, but first and foremost I value candor. "Well," I started, "I've got a bit of virtual teaching experience under my belt now. It'll never replace traditional instruction, but I feel that it's grown on me. I've still managed to form those connections with my students even in a remote atmosphere, and I've made a lot of adaptations to the new technology. I could see myself really doing well and enjoying myself in a remote teaching situation."

There was a short pause, and a "hmm". I could picture her on the other end of the call with her hand scratching her chin, and her feet tapping against the floor.

Finally, she concluded, "All right. I'll tell you what: we'll give you an interview and we can sit down and chat about it." Arranging a time for an interview was an effortless task, given my natural presence in the building for the leadership of my summer camp sessions. Their typical group interviewing style involved having potential candidates answering a pre-customized set of prompts in front of a panel stacked with others such as teachers and specialists in addition to themselves. Fortunately, since I had already undergone one of these dreadful group style interviews, they decided that my virtual academy interview would be more intimate. The panel would only consist of my two administrators.

The three of us sat at the long rectangular table in the main office conference room where most small group meetings were held. I nervously rocked back and forth in my chair, while profusely tapping my black BIC pen, adjusting my collar multiple times, and picking at the green bracelet attached to my right wrist. My principal began, "We decided that there's really no point in asking the same questions we already asked you in the group interview. So, here's what we're going to do… We have two positions open. First, we're going to share with you details about each and what our reservations are. Then, you'll get a chance to present your points and discuss your feelings about possibly serving in one of these roles." My anxiety level plummeted and a feeling of tranquility swept over me like a soothing fall breeze.

The two women began diving into specifics. "The first virtual opening is in third grade. Currently, there are thirty students enrolled and so far, seven have IEPs and receive special education services. The second option is fifth grade. As of this moment, we have twenty-six students enrolled in this section. Six of these students are identified with disabilities and are entitled to special education services. One of these six students is on a modified curriculum. Do you understand what a modified curriculum would look like in this situation?" asked my principal.

"I've never taught a student who's been on a modified curriculum, but I feel that my skills and training have prepared me to deal with a scenario like this," I replied earnestly. I felt quite apprehensive about the prospect of teaching a student on modified curriculum and the liability it presented.

My interviewers were transparent about their hesitancy to place a novice teacher in a setting with needs this high. "We're aware of how challenging both of these roles are," my principal proceeded. "Quite frankly, we're even hesitant to hire a seasoned teacher into one of these positions. That being said, now that we've shared our reservations and feelings about these two positions with you, we do have another potential opening."

"Yes," my assistant principal chimed in. "We've noticed how you've gotten really involved with the STEM camps this summer, so we think this prospective role might be good for you." My assistant principal explained further, "A contract role we're hoping to obtain funding for involves leading STEM activities with small groups of students. We feel that this might be a really good opportunity for a first-year teacher. It would still utilize your talents, and I think this would be a good starting point for you to develop your skills. So, that's all from our end. Now, what are your feelings?"

I already knew which of the three options appealed most to me. "Well, after listening to all the details, I feel that I'm the best fit for the fifth-grade virtual opening," I began. "I don't claim to be a special education expert by any means, but I have worked in inclusion settings with very high needs. The ratio of students with IEPs is comparable to what you're describing in this virtual position. In these roles, I learned how to address an array of different learning needs, how to collect data toward students' IEP goals, and how to implement IEPs. Plus, I have a really good rapport with our educational diagnostician. I'll work closely with her, I won't hesitate to clarify any details with her, and I'll check in with her frequently. I'm not afraid to ask for help and use my resources. I'm also aware of how much liability is involved here, and I'm not ignorant of the ramifications of shitting the bed with spec ed."

Both of my prospective bosses glanced at one another, nodded and smiled. However, I had not thoroughly convinced them yet. So, I moved straight in to my next marketing point. "There's something I can offer you that even a veteran may not be able to," I boldly asserted. "The fifth-grade math strategies for common core are very intimidating and tricky for a lot of teachers, even ones with years of experience. Especially when it comes to the fraction skills for fifth grade, you can smell the fear. But this is where my roots are. You see, I have a background as a title one tutor in my old district. I led fourth and fifth grade math intervention groups, and it was my job to work with small groups of struggling students on these math concepts. I lived and breathed all the different common core math strategies and that's literally what I did all day long. I was trained to use hands-on manipulatives and concrete representations in this job. If I could help fill these kids' holes and get results then, I feel that I can use my math background in this position too. I know that some of these concepts, especially the fractions skills, aren't just going to automatically click for my six friends with IEPs. This is something that I'm used to dealing with, and I can get through to them."

My interviewers leaned back in their chairs and nodded. "How do you feel about teaching in a virtual environment? What about all the technology you'll have to manage? Is this really something you want?" they asked me.

"I'll be perfectly honest," I said. "Before I had any exposure to remote teaching, I was scared shitless. I wanted to run for the hills, and I thought it'd be a horrible experience. The first weeks of my virtual teaching experience were a nightmare." I continued, "But then, I started to acclimate to the new technology, and everything began to run more smoothly. I also explored new ways to build relationships remotely, and I realized that I can cultivate relationships with my kids online just as I would in a regular classroom. You both know that technology is one area that I really want to grow in professionally. This would be the perfect opportunity for me to become more tech savvy. I learn something best when I'm in a situation that forces me to either know it or drown," I said, grinning.

I also felt I should remind them of some of the storms I had weathered. "Look. You made me the educator I am by tossing me into a bunch of shituations," I said. Both of their faces turned red as they roared with laughter at my blunt remark. They knew that I was alluding to two particular long-term substitute roles that I took on prior to the strike of the zombie apocalypse, where I stepped into frenzy islands. "If I can walk into a bad shituation in the middle of the year, fix it and turn it around, then I can certainly walk into a clean slate at the beginning of the year and do an even better job," I proceeded.

I then referred back to my assistant principal's earlier comment about her vision of me in the STEM role. "I realize the STEM job is where you think I fit best, but I really think I'm better off in the fifth-grade virtual role." I asserted. "In a hypothetical scenario where you gave me the choice between the two, I'd pick the fifth-grade virtual class, hands-down. I really want the opportunity to have the impact of making a difference in the lives of a group of kids. I really won't get that chance if

I'm in a role where I only work with small groups of kids for half an hour a few times each week. Having the consistency of being with a full class of students all day long allows me to build strong relationships that I wouldn't be able to build in the short time I'd have with my STEM groups. Plus, I really feel that fifth grade is an age level where a lot of our kids really need a positive male role model. I want to be that role model for them."

We then exchanged some closing remarks, and I headed on my way to the district office to attend a substitute teacher training. Since I had no guarantee of securing this position yet, I wanted to maintain my backup plan. The two administrators knew where I was heading. As I was heading out the door of the conference room, my principal called to me, "Oh, by the way, we'll still have several long-term substitute positions open this year too." The sound of this comment striking my ear caused my gut to churn. That night, I tossed and turned underneath the covers for several hours before I was finally able to fall asleep. I woke to a text the next morning from the two women. The message read: *Good morning! We were really impressed with how you presented your points yesterday and how you sold yourself yesterday. That being said, we cannot confirm or deny at this point that a position is being offered. However, if you were offered the position as our fifth-grade virtual teacher, what would you add onto the already existing school supply list for your students?*

I immediately felt a sense of joy, as adrenaline rushed through my body. I responded to the group text with a few additional items that I felt my students would need. I also provided an explanation for each of these items and described how I would have students utilize them. Shortly after, I received a simple: *Thank you!*

My intuition that I was being offered the position was confirmed three days later when I received the official phone call from the human resources recruiting supervisor. "Congratulations!" he exclaimed. "You're now officially a teacher in our district!" I jumped out of my seat and threw my hands up into the air with glee.

"Can you please repeat that one more time?" I implored him.

"You are *officially* a teacher in this district!" he reiterated, with a light chuckle.

"Wow! Thank you so much! This is the best news ever!" I cried. I was eager to share my news.

I called one of my close friends who'd worked in her local school system for several years. "I got the job!" I boomed with excitement.

"Congratulations!" she said. "So, how do you feel about your new position?"

I shared my honest feelings with her. "Well, I'm thrilled. I got fifth grade, which is exactly what I wanted! It's a great fit for me! The only thing I'm nervous about, is the number of kids with IEPs in my class."

"How many do you have?" she asked curiously.

"Looks like I'm going to have six, one of those is on a modified curriculum." I explained.

"Six?" she repeated in shock. "You have six kids with special education needs in a virtual classroom? That's insane! How do they think that they're supposed to be able to get what they need to be successful in a virtual setting? They can't possibly think that it's a good idea to put six kids with IEPs online who already struggle to learn in a regular classroom as it is."

I could not dispute the logic. "Honestly, I can't say that it is a good idea. I haven't even started this quest yet. I've still got more questions than I've got answers myself. But you know what: I've been tossed into a lot of shituations, and I've always found a way to survive. I just feel like somehow, this won't be any different; I'll find my way like I always have."

My other main concern, as anyone who knows me would easily predict, was adapting to all the dreaded technology. I tried to view the technological aspect of my job with a positive outlook. *This will force me to overcome my paralyzing fear of technology once and for all,* I rationalized. I was certainly not incorrect. The number of opportunities to achieve my professional growth goal of furthering my proficiency with technology would be limitless, as I would soon experience.

Blast Off

(August 2021)

The beginning of the school year was like a rocket exploding into outer space. Careful planning and thoughtful designs cannot prevent chaos whenever all hell decides to break loose without warning or hesitation. In this particular instance, bedlam decided to manifest itself in the form of a gigantic staff shortage.

Before this year, I believed that the so called 'teacher shortage' was merely a fabricated myth. Afterall, I had waited two years after completion of my student teaching in this district to finally acquire a contracted role. A team meeting that took place at the end of August with my principal and assistant principal, prior to students' return to school, proved to be quite enlightening.

My assistant principal was sharing some interesting details. "We're seeing a teacher shortage this year like never before. It's crazy – we just can't get people any more. A ton of teachers are all deciding to retire at once. We've lost of people because they don't want to risk their health teaching with COVID around. We're not sure how we're going to have enough people to fill positions this year, especially regarding virtual academy. It's almost September at this point and we're still short staffed." I was taken aback by this news.

"I've been trying to get in this district for the last two years," I exclaimed. "Internal competition had made it nearly impossible for me to even be eligible for an interview." I mentioned how on the rare occasion that a posting was open to external applicants, there would be roughly two hundred and fifty applicants aside from me with years of experience and impressive degrees.

"Well, that's definitely not the case any more. Internal applicants aren't even wanting to transfer here any more. As a matter of fact, we just interviewed several internal candidates for a position and offered it to all of them, none of them accepted it, believe it or not."

Many teachers, particularly veterans with decades of experience, decided to grab hold of their pensions and flee from all of the new technology and dodge the obstacles that a brand-new learning platform presented. Others grew impatient with the inconsistency of alternating between teaching on Zoom and teaching in-person. Of course, there were also a group of educators who decided to depart for health and safety reasons, fearing the risk of endangering themselves and their families.

This left my administration in the precarious position of contending with the reality that the ratio of the projected growth rate of teachers to the projected growth rate of new students entering the district would be disproportionate. To make matters worse, this inconvenience was compounded with one minor flaw in the rollout of our virtual academy.

The generous open-door policy for new enrollments in our district's virtual academy had no existing expiration date, and there was no deadline for registration of new pupils. At the last moment, registration requests continued to flood the office with a surge greater than that of Hurricane Katrina. Of course, these were more or less *requests*. Not a single application was denied. I assume that my administration probably felt like genies, as they were required to grant the wishes of every family who wished to enroll late. Despite hiring fifteen new staff members at the beginning of the school year, a new record for my school, these efforts were still insufficient to withstand the tsunami of students entering our academy.

In our beginning of year virtual team meeting, my assistant principal continued to explain the crisis at hand. "We have a lot of internal staffing challenges on our hands right now. One of our third-grade virtual teachers is about to go out on maternity leave for twelve weeks. She's not the only one – one of our in our in-person fourth grade teachers is also expecting soon too. We don't have enough long-term subs to choose from, and the ones we already have we're using right now." She sighed. "Our back-up plan is no good either: the one teacher we were going to pull from in person to make her virtual is now going to be out most of the year for an illness."

I looked at her and said, "It's too bad you can't use me as a long-term sub any more."

She laughed and nodded. "True." she agreed. One can logically deduce that when a teacher and paraprofessional shortage already exists, naturally a concurrent shortage of substitutes to fill these vacancies inherently exists as well. Therefore, the circumstances were even less optimal than originally anticipated.

With only one virtual class per grade level, class sizes spiked to an all-time high. During our team meeting, another one of the items my principal and vice-principal had on our agenda to cover was discussion of the enrollment numbers for each class.

"So, it looks like third and fourth grade are the high fliers here," my principal revealed. "Right now, both of these grades are up to fifty kids. Right now, we don't have any support for you, so you'll be starting the year solo." she explained to those two teachers. "As soon as we're able to get an extra para and one of our teachers comes back from maternity leave, we'll be able to add some support to your rooms." Dialogue was exchanged, and one of the teachers raised an unforeseen concern.

"The breakout room features of Zoom don't allow for a number of students this high," she articulated. She was correct. Zoom imposed a maximum cap of fifty students for utilization of small group and individual breakout rooms. This would prove problematic, especially considering the number of students in these classes whose IEPs entitled them to receive a specified amount of small group instruction time each week.

While my virtual reality was less challenging than that of three of my colleagues, it certainly qualified as a close runner up. "How many students am I up to on my roster as of this moment?" I asked both of my new bosses.

"As of right now, you're up to forty-two," my principal replied. "And just to level with you, you're probably last on the list to for extra support. Third and fourth grade have the highest numbers, so they're going to be prioritized over fifth grade." I knew this meant that I would most likely be flying solo for several months and I was correct.

I kept my cool, and refused to let my mindset be soured by what I was about to face. I had prevailed in several shituations leading up to this one. So, I simply declared this to be nothing more than an ordinary shituation which would be yet another milestone in developing my grit as an educator. However, the uncertainty of what lay ahead kept my mind stirring constantly. Already an insomniac since childhood, this was definitely posing a challenge for The Sandman.

I took Labor Day weekend to prepare for my first week with students. They were coming, all forty-two of them, and I would be ready. I planned several introductory activities, and assembled my special education binder, where I would keep all my records of students' data samples and progress toward their IEP goals.

Edutainment

(September 2021)

During the first week of school, the challenge at hand was great: keep forty-two kids engaged on screen for six and a half hours each day, with only an hour break for lunch and recess. Even as a mature, grounded, college-educated adult, I wondered how I myself could even manage this amount of daily screen time. I felt empathy and compassion for these kids – and of course, for myself as well. The first week was critical. Somehow, I had to captivate these young minds, and quickly, in order to set the foundation for the entire year.

It was time to get creative. I drew from the tool bag of ideas that I had acquired from my previous experiences and from the many mentors I had worked with over the past few years. I also reflected back on my own school experiences from childhood, and allowed my nostalgia to guide my planning as well.

One fond memory that I had from my elementary school days was when my teachers read aloud the *Wayside School* series by Louis Sachar to my classmates and I. They read to us with such energy and enthusiasm that I still remember being eager to come inside from recess and sit down on the carpet to hear the next chapter. Seating my remote students down on a carpet in front of me while I watched their reactions up close was not an option for me this year. Nevertheless, I realized that a charismatic read aloud was still a powerful tool that I could deploy in a virtual setting.

I incorporated these read-alouds into my students' daily routine. I enjoyed getting into character and practicing my method acting skills on camera. Being raised by a reading specialist, I learned to alternate my vocal stylings in order to do impressions for each of the different characters in the story.

The first chapter of the first book in the series required me to impersonate Mrs. Gorf, the meanest teacher ever to walk the halls of Wayside who turned her children into apples. For this, I brought out my high-pitched, nails on a chalkboard, wicked witch voice. There was also a character named Paul, who was addicted to the sensation he received from constantly yanking his classmate Leslie's pigtails, which tempted and tantalized Paul as they dangled in front of him. My pigtail voice was a high-pitched whisper voice, comparable to a voice one might use when coaxing a baby to stop crying. My Mr. Kidswatter voice was one of the easiest and most fun. He was the authoritarian principal of Wayside School, who was widely unpopular amongst the student body. For him, I would simply just deepen my voice, making myself sound like an intimidating drill sergeant. The most difficult character for me to portray was Mr. Gorf, the son of Mrs. Gorf, who posed as a substitute teacher for the children on the thirtieth story on a covert mission to seek revenge upon them for causing his dear mother to vanish. Sachar described the sound of Mr. Gorf's actual voice as a congested donkey. It was impossible to manage this impression without a full glass of water sitting next to me the entire time. Read aloud time was a major hit with my class. It is still the time of day that they eagerly anticipate and look forward to the most. However, read alouds were just one of the tools I had at my disposal.

The variety of games that are suited for a remote learning

environment is surprisingly wide. Kahoots are not only a great check for understanding at the end of a lesson, but they were also a great tool for me to use for my first week of school introductory and 'getting to know you' activities. My students loved this timed, quiz-like game with suspenseful music and captivating backgrounds. Even in a digital era though, good old-fashioned games that involve no electronics can still have an equally potent impact.

Two Truths And a Lie was a simple, yet exciting activity that allowed me to build a strong classroom community and hold my students' interest during those first days of school. I began first by sharing two statements about myself that were true and one that was false. My class then had to take their best shot at guessing which of the three statements was the lie. Of course, my fifth graders were sharp enough to quickly identify the statement that was false. Then, each of my students were given a turn to drop their three statements into the chatroom, and everyone else had to guess what their lie was. Not only did my students learn more about me and one another, but they also tremendously enjoyed the activity. Of course, fun and engaging activities were effective; however, there are always instances where students need additional motivation and positive reinforcement.

My school established a building wide ticket economy system which had been in place prior to the strike of the zombie apocalypse. Students could earn tickets and cash them in for various rewards. The only dilemma with applying this ticket system within a virtual setting was that most rewards offered were only feasible in a traditional, in-person setting. Adapting the ticket economy idea to my virtual classroom required some creative thinking. I invested time into brainstorming some ideas for potential rewards that some of my students would still enjoy online. I had my students contribute ideas as well.

It turned out that the simplest privileges had the greatest impact. "So guys, what are some of the rewards you might like to have for your loyalty tickets? Remember, it has to work in our remote setting." I explained.

One of the students raised her hand on Zoom. "I'd like to be able to earn the privilege of being co-host on Zoom for the day." Surprisingly, this would initially be a very popular choice when my students redeemed their tickets. Having the ability to admit other students into the meeting, jump in between different breakout rooms, and assist me with spotlighting the view of classmates who were speaking provided them with a sense of leadership. I let the ideas from my students flow.

Another student suggested, "Let's have some extra Wayside School read aloud." I lit up when I heard this request.

"Most definitely! If someone cashes in forty tickets, everyone gets to hear one extra chapter. If someone redeems sixty, I'll read two!"

My students were delighted by my response. One of them spoke up, "We're all going to band together one day, like on a Friday afternoon or right before a break. Then, we'll all cash in our loyalty tickets at the exact same time and keep making you read to us so we can get out of having to any work for the rest of the day." This later would come to fruition, the day before an extended break.

I recall one particular instance on the last day preceding a long weekend when four students conspired to elude any regular instruction for the second half of the day. They continued cashing in their tickets until the day was over and I completely finished the current book I was reading to them in the Wayside School series. There was also one particular student who found amusement in watching me make a goober out of myself.

For a very high number of tickets, I promised students that they could earn the opportunity to hear me speak in a special accent for a full day. This one young lady finally took me up on my offer. So, I prepared myself to jump into character and embraced my inner thespian. I chose the accent of an Alabama corn and soybean farmer. I even went one step further by renaming myself on Zoom, and calling myself 'Farmer'. I attempted to teach my normal lessons as planned, but getting my students to take me seriously that day was quite difficult. Half of them could not stop laughing long enough to concentrate, and the other half complained, "We can't understand a single word you're saying! Nothing makes sense when you talk in that weird voice!" I did not mind stepping out of my comfort zone and even embarrassing myself a bit. If it meant that it would be appreciated by my students and it would offer incentive for them to actively participate in the virtual learning environment, I was more than willing to offer them a laugh at my expense.

I am continuing to realize not only how important it is to keep my students feeling excited about their online learning experience, but also how challenging it can be to do so at times. A student's level of enthusiasm can drop in the blink of an eye, whenever a minor hiccup or an unpleasant experience presents itself.

My first week was a pleasant, but brief honeymoon period. The rest of September would be a month of woes, filled with stress.

First Month Woes

(September 2021)

I expected the first few weeks of school to be a seamless transition to a new school year. What I experienced that first month felt like the polar opposite. Having to withstand the testing and technology nightmares nearly drove me to my wits end. Then of course, there were the snow plow mom, the streaker, and the misandrist. These were my beginning of year endurance tests.

During the month of September, I was required to administer several different beginning of year assessments. All of the late and last-minute enrollments in our virtual academy meant roughly half of my students were not yet in possession of their district issued technology, or did not have their necessary software updates completed. MAP, one particular assessment that I was required to administer at the beginning of the year for the purpose of measuring growth and monitoring students' trouble spots overtime, was the bane of my existence.

The window provided for MAP administration was rigid and tight. I had never administered this test before in person, let alone via Zoom. Thinking that I had taken all necessary steps to be proactive and prevent chaos from ensuing, I confidently began the first round of MAP testing with my students. Within fifteen minutes, I was in an utter panic and frantically pleading with the main office to track down the geek squad for me.

Half of my class had their yellow hand icons raised on

Zoom. They were all demanding my attention at once. Several students complained, "I have a blank white screen! My computer monitor looks like a snowstorm!"

Others were calling out to me, "My name is not showing up on the menu. I keep scrolling down to find it, but it's not here!"

A few were also telling me, "We can't get the app to work for our test! It's not loading properly!" Meanwhile, my phone was blowing up with texts and my inbox was being inundated with emails from confused and frustrated parents who could not figure out how to help their children log on to the test.

One parent called me on the phone, frantic. "Excuse me, sir, we can't get this test to work. We've been trying for the last half hour to get in, but we can't!"

In the midst of hyperventilating and my hands shaking as they pressed against the keyboard, I replied, "I'm not sure how to fix all these problems. The best I can tell you for now is to power the device off and then reboot it and try again. Hopefully, they'll be sending some help soon."

"Well, I *hope* its soon – like I said, it's already been over half an hour." remarked the parent. At this point my face was beat red from my elevated blood pressure, and beads of sweat were dripping down my forehead.

The panic and demands for my attention and technological assistance, which I was incapable of providing, continued coming forth. Finally, one student made a comment that was the last straw for me. "I'm so sick of the stupid thing not working! I feel like all we've done this whole week is test, test, test! When is all this stupid testing going to be over? When am I going to get a freakin' iPad that works?"

I finally snapped. "Everyone, just cool it!" I boomed. "There's forty-two of you, and only one of me! You're just going to have to suck it up and be patient! I'm not Superman, and I can't solve everybody's problem at once! This stupid MAP system is a pain in the butt, and it's not my fault it won't work!" After my rant, I heard the sound of keys wrangling, and my door swung open. It was the geek squad to the rescue.

I placed myself on mute to vent. "Dude, I swear to God, I'm ready to jump out of this mother fucking window right now!" I ranted, pointing to the window behind my desk.

"Oh no! We can't have you do that!" He laughed. "What's going wrong with MAP?"

"Everything!" I exclaimed.

"All right, let's just take it one test a time here... Who's having issues?" I ran down the list with him of students encountering various problems. He jumped into my rolling chair behind my computer monitor, and jumped into action.

"Okay, let's see... aha! You need to just go to the app store and redownload the app, and then you'll be good!" he told the first student. "I'll show you how here, real quick; go ahead and share your screen." The geek squad worked his magic with each student and within fifteen minutes everyone had successfully begun their assessments.

"I don't know how the hell you do it, man." I said to him.

"It's all good. It's your first time doing this and you're doing it remotely, which is a nightmare."

I took a deep breath. "I need some fucking Advil or ibuprofen right about now. You got one you can spare me?" I asked. Fortunately, the geek squad is always armed and prepared.

Henceforth, I vowed to always keep a bottle of ibuprofen handy in my desk drawer during MAP testing week. The geek squad had to practically live in my Zoom room until I survived that week of pure testing hell. Meanwhile, I had a relentless snowplow mom personally riding my bumper.

There was one student in my class whose mother felt entitled to have a special set of rules and expectations for her child. Work completion and class participation were not something that her daughter, who I nicknamed Dizzy, took a particular fancy to. I would describe this child with the same phrase that Dr. Otto Octavius used to describe Peter Parker in *Spider Man 2*: 'brilliant, but lazy'. A virtual learning placement further enabled the snowplow mom and her daughter to evade accountability.

One day, I was reviewing directions for an assignment. "Okay guys: so, you're going to solve these problems on Classkick. Here's the link," I said, as I dropped the assignment link into the chatroom. "I'm also going to write the directions in the chat, in case you forget what we're doing." I told my class. I then assigned them to individual breakout rooms to complete the task at hand. One marvelous benefit of utilizing Classkick, is the ability to watch my students working in live time which saves me the headache of having to bounce to different breakout rooms. Dizzy had not even begun her first slide, and had not even clicked the link. I had been noticing this pattern for nearly two weeks, and I was fed up.

I bounced into her breakout room. Her camera was turned off and her microphone was muted. I called her name once, and received no response. "Where are you?" I demanded. "I need you to flip your video on and answer me, right now! You may be at home, but this is still school and you can't just get up and wander away whenever you feel like it!"

Finally, she appeared on camera with a dazed look of bewilderment. "Huh? W-w-what?" she stammered.

"What are you doing? Why have you been sitting in here doing nothing?" I growled impatiently.

"W-w-what?" she once again managed to utter.

"You need to be on Classkick! You can't just be sitting here doing nothing!" I scolded.

"We're supposed to be doing something?" she asked, bamboozled.

"I gave directions twice *and* I wrote them in the chat." I responded.

"O-oh."

At this point, I was growing quite annoyed. I took a deep breath. "Where were you when I was giving directions?"

"I guess I just wasn't listening when you gave directions." she admitted.

"No, I guess not," I agreed. I repeated directions to her once again, and directed her back on task. Still, another thirty minutes managed to elapse without her completing a single slide. I pulled her aside in a breakout room.

"You have not finished a single assignment since the beginning of the school year!" I told her. "What do you expect at report card time if you don't turn in any work?"

"I don't know!" she whined. "I-I-I just—this is all too much for me! I'm so confused. I don't understand! I'm not sure what I'm supposed to do! I have no clue!" She raised her voice.

"You know what, that's it! I'm calling your mom!" I told her. On Saturday that weekend, I decided to dial Dizzy's mother, since I had not even a moment to breath during the week. I expected her to side with my logic and reasoning; however, I quickly discovered that I was wasting my time.

Dizzy's snowplow mother did not feel the inclination to even allow me to finish a complete sentence, before abruptly cutting me off. "Have you reviewed her 504 accommodations?" she asked sharply.

"Yes, ma'am. I have and I see here—" I was once again interrupted.

"She gets extended time on assignments." snapped the snowplow mom.

"I'm well aware," I explained. "However, I feel like the line between extended time and unlimited time is getting blurred here."

Snowplow mom scoffed. "What's *that* supposed to mean?" she snarled.

"I mean, she hasn't completed even one single assignment since we've been in school so far. Her accommodation for extended time gives her one and a half of the time which other students get. For example, if the rest of the class gets an hour—"

"I can do the math," she retorted. "My problem here is, how does she know when she's allowed to finish the assignments?"

"I beg your pardon?" I asked in utter bamboozlement. "If you don't tell her that she's allowed to keep working, she doesn't know." I was astounded by this ridiculous comment. "I *expect* her to keep working until she's finishes the assignment, which I've made crystal clear."

There was a long awkward pause. Then snowplow mom asked me, "How long have you taught? Is this your first year?" she asked me.

"Yes. It is my first year, but I've undergone a lot of training for this job, I went to school for it, and I'm not new to this district. I've long-term subbed for years," I explained.

"Ah, I thought you were a newbie," she continued. "You know, I think it would be helpful if you shared your lesson plans with me. I would be intrigued to have a look at them." I almost had to pick my jaw up off of the floor from the audacity of this woman.

"I'm sorry, ma'am, but it's not policy for teachers to disclose their lesson plans with parents. I've never had a parent ask me that before, and I'm pretty certain none of my colleagues have ever been asked that by a parent either. Our administrators don't even ask us to turn in daily plans for inspection. Out of curiosity, why would you need my daily lesson plans?"

"Oh, I just figure that they might be helpful since you're teaching my child. They might help me understand what you're teaching, how you're teaching it, and what you're expecting her to do." she replied.

I chuckled. "Well, I can assure you, I make my expectations very clear in class and I adhere to my curriculum guides when I prepare and teach my lessons. So not to worry: your daughter's in good hands."

Still dissatisfied, the mother suggested, "Well, maybe you can just send me the graded assignments that she has to do a week or two in advance so that I can be on it and help her stay on task."

I was tempted to hang up the phone at this point. "Unfortunately, I can't do that. Plus, I don't always know for a fact which specific day I'm going to give a graded assignment because I'm flexible based on the needs in my class." I explained.

"Uh-hu." replied the snowplow mom. "Well, you could at least provide a checklist. Her teacher last year always gave her a checklist of the assignments she had to turn in every day."

I reminded to her, "A checklist isn't necessary, because all she has to do is look in the Schoology folders for each subject every day and it says right in there what she's expected to submit. It even displays the directions and time it's due."

Since I was already on a roll, I decided to proceed. "Also, I noticed that her camera is off most of the day. She doesn't answer me when I call her name. So, that's indicating to me that she's probably not always listening or paying attention when I'm going over directions."

"Have you made her aware that you expect her to keep her camera on?" the snowplow mom asked.

I replied, "Yes. I definitely have, many times. I enforce this for every student."

Looking for a way to save face, she then asked, "Do you have that expectation posted for them somewhere in writing – like on Schoology, maybe?"

I almost felt as though I was being interrogated by a paralegal.

"No, it's not on Schoology. But, it is written in the contract that was signed at the beginning of the year when you enrolled her in the virtual academy." As I was speaking, I located the electronic copy of the virtual academy agreement and directly quoted the line stating that students were required to keep their cameras on.

"She feels very self-conscious about having to be visible to all her classmates every moment," argued snowplow mom. "It makes her very uncomfortable. When she feels like she's being judged or under a microscope for other kids to see, it makes her anxiety worse and she can't concentrate as well."

I was now flipping snowplow mom off through the phone. "I do understand that but, on the other hand, I really feel that her being invisible makes me unable to help her stay on task."

"Okay but just so you understand, she hates being called out in front of the entire class. When you say to her 'please flip your video on' in front of all her classmates, she gets really embarrassed and says it makes her feel super weird and uncomfortable," the snowplow mom rebutted.

"It's not my intention to make her feel the least bit

uncomfortable," I explained. "But I have to get her attention somehow. When I need to see a student's face, I ask them nicely to turn their camera on. If I pulled every student into a breakout room individually every time I needed them to make themselves visible on screen, I wouldn't have time to get any instruction in."

"I totally get that," replied the snowplow mom. "But just keep in mind that she's sensitive, I think you can agree that every child's feelings matter."

Clenching my fists, I said, "Yes, my students' feelings are *very* important to me." I was feeling like I had had enough of this conversation. "Look, I don't mean to cut you short, but I actually need to go." I stated, in an attempt to salvage what was remaining of my Saturday evening. I had spent nearly two hours in total on the phone with the snowplow mom, yielding absolutely no positive results.

My communications with this snowplow mom were never shy of awkward; however, having to communicate with the mother of my nudist student to let her know about her son's naked state, definitely qualifies for a category of its own.

One gentleman in my class either detested clothing with a passion or was an aspiring model. Although he had unshaken confidence and took great pride in his naked state, nobody else relished in his displays. My principal and I especially did not appreciate the imagery.

Beginning the second week of school, he appeared on camera laying down sideways. He had a blue blanket thrown over his head, but he wore no shirt. His plaid boxer shorts were visible, along with his naked chest and torso. The first day I noticed this, I pulled him into a breakout room to speak with him.

"I just want to remind you of our classroom expectations. You need to be dressed on Zoom every day, which means you need to be wearing a shirt and pants. Pajamas won't work either, and neither will a blanket." He rolled his eyes, groaned, and did not utter a word. "Do you understand?" I asked him.

"Yeah, whatever," he mumbled.

"You better be dressed tomorrow!" I warned him. I decided to have a follow-up conversation with my principal.

"It looks like I have a friend in my class who's a little confused, he must think it's still summer vacation and that he's on the beach, because he's been showing up on Zoom half naked every day."

My principal's face became contorted with disgust. "That's not okay!" she exclaimed. "If he comes in like that again, you need to let me know!"

"Believe me, I sure will," I assured her.

Surely enough, the next day he once again appeared on Zoom with the same blue blanket thrown over his head, laying sideways still, and mostly disrobed. I texted my principal the moment I took notice. About five minutes later, I heard the ding sound which notifies me when someone shows up in my Zoom waiting room. It was my principal. I admitted her into the meeting.

"Good morning," she greeted me. "Would you please go ahead and make me co-host of your meeting so I can meet with one of your students in a breakout room?" I did as she instructed, and she met with the student. Shortly afterward, he returned fully dressed, sitting up straight. My principal followed up with me later.

"So, I talked to that friend of yours. I also went ahead and sent an email to his mom, which I cc'd you in. Tomorrow, you shouldn't have this issue with him again. If you do, let me know please." I nodded in agreement. "By the way, he has no clue that you told me anything. He and his mother will just be under the impression that I happened to be in your Zoom observing and that I noticed this while I was in there." I hoped that the young nudist had finally gotten the message. Unfortunately, the message was still failing to sink in.

The very next day, he entered my Zoom disrobed, plaid boxers, his eyes half open. I once again yanked out my cell phone and messaged my principal, who came into my virtual classroom once again. She met with the young streaker a second time, and followed up with the single parent once more. Still, he either really took pride in his state of nakedness or just was quite stubborn. The antics continued for the next few weeks.

My principal and assistant principal each took turns popping into my Zoom room to meet with him and reach out to his mother. This was an ongoing battle that we continued to fight throughout the entire month of September. However, this was not the only battle that I fought during my first month of this new adventure.

One morning as I had just dismissed students for their lunch and recess break, my classroom wall phone rang. It was my virtual registrar. "Hey! I just got off the phone with a parent. She's indignant. She was very upset and has some concerns. She was trying to explain everything to me, but I told her that she really needs to take it up with you since you're the teacher."

"Who's the parent?" I asked. When she revealed who it was, I was utterly confused. "I'm really surprised to hear that this lady is upset. I mean, I can't really think of any reason why she'd have a problem with me. Her daughter and I haven't had any issues or run ins. She's not failing anything. I haven't scolded her or corrected her for anything, either. I really don't get what her issue is."

"Well, when you get a chance, just go ahead and give her a

ring – I'm sure she'll tell you herself." the registrar explained. During my lunch period, I dialed the parent on my phone which was attached to the wall across from my sink. I quickly learned the cause of her hostility when I reached out to the woman myself.

"Good morning," I greeted the woman. "I understand you have some concerns you wanted to discuss with me?" I asked gently.

"Yes, I certainly do," she replied. "You see, I don't think—no offense—but I really don't believe that you are the right person to be teaching elementary school."

"Oh, I'm so sorry you feel that way. If I've done anything to offend you or your daughter, I sincerely apologize. But I really do—" I was interrupted.

"Well, it's not so much that it's your teaching. It's really just that men don't have what it takes to teach kids this age. I mean you *guys* just have no patience, and you're not nurturing toward young children."

Extremely offended, I bit my lip and took a deep breath before I continued speaking. "With all due respect, I believe that's a bit of a hasty generalization, ma'am," I rebutted calmly. "In this day and age, the number of male educators at the elementary school level has significantly increased. My gender has nothing to do with the quality of my work, or my passion. I care deeply about my students and my craft." I explained to this misandrist.

"Yeah, I-I mean, I do sense that about you. But, you know, it's kind of obvious that male teachers are better off with older students. To tell you the truth, when I first heard she was going to have a man teaching this year, I was like, oh my God! I couldn't believe my ears!" she said. At this point, I could not believe my own ears.

"Okay. Aside from that, are there any other concerns you want to speak to me about?" I asked her.

"Um, I—uh—I think, well, I do have one other thing. How come my daughter isn't being awarded any tickets?" she sputtered. I pulled out my sheet and glanced at the total number of tickets listed next to her name. "According to my records here, she has forty-five."

The misandrist was still dissatisfied. "Oh, well—well, how come the other students have more?"

Fortunately, I was able to easily refute the baseless case she was attempting to build against me. "On my sheet here, I can tell you that the highest number of tickets any student has earned at this point is sixty-seven." I explained to the woman.

"How do they earn these tickets?" she demanded.

"It's based on a variety of different factors: participation, perseverance on assignments, winning games in class, working well with classmates in their breakout rooms, and a variety of other ways too." I replied.

"Um, okay." she stammered.

"Anything else?" I asked.

"I-I think I've covered my concerns for today." she said. I heard a click and she was off the phone line.

By the dawn of October, everything had finally begun to settle down. My students and I were acclimated to a simple routine of organized chaos. Technology was finally working, and I was finally gaining a firm handle on it. Each of my students had their school iPads with all their apps and updates, and almost a day managed to elapse without me receiving a technology related parent text message or email. This was a remarkable accomplishment for me, one I deemed worthy of celebration.

In surrender, the young male model finally began appearing in a clothed state *most* days of the week, much to his resentment. Snowplow mom and I finally reached a mutual understanding, and her daughter was required to complete the assigned classwork which she greatly abhorred. *All these massive victories in only one month of school,* I joked.

In addition, I achieved what I believed to be another major breakthrough. One of my primary concerns entering into this role was being able to fully accommodate and satisfy the needs of my students with IEPs. The ability to have access to hands-on math manipulative tools and for them to be consistently embedded into the instruction they received was one accommodation which each of their IEPs explicitly stated they were entitled to. Being in a remote setting, I feared that I would fall short due to the fact that any type of hands-on activities are almost impossible to plan and implement.

Afterall, I knew since orientation week that I would be unable to conduct any of the science experiments with my students which were the 'meat and potatoes' of my district's science curriculum. Instead, I was forced to reduce these originally exciting and engaging lessons to mere on-screen teacher led demonstrations. I am sure the students were as equally thrilled about this watered-down version of the science curriculum as I was. However, lo and behold, there was a solution for math: virtual manipulatives.

My district's curriculum provided an additional website that armed teachers with math apps that they could provide to students. Digital base ten blocks were available to offer a concrete visual model for crucial concepts such as decimals, a key concept expected to be mastered in fifth grade. I was also enamored with the digital money pieces and the digital math clocks that were provided, as they would prove themselves to be instrumental when teaching several fraction concepts. For example, having students relate basic fractions to a number of minutes on the clock armed them with an additional strategy to rely on.

My students with special education needs were the greatest benefactors of these brilliant resources. When grading my periodic checkpoints and the end of unit assessment on fractions, these students demonstrated drastic leaps and bounds. One student in particular, who had struggled immensely with math and who had historically scored within the lowest percentile on math assessments, scored within the highest percentile of my entire class on this unit test. He showed an improvement of three letter grades from what he typically scored on math assessments.

To enhance the effectiveness of these digital math tools, I took full advantage of Classkick's live time feature. By creating Classkick slides for my students with the manipulatives embedded into these slides, I was able to observe each of my students interacting with the manipulatives step by step, in any given moment. Coming from my not tech savvy background, I felt like I had been transported through time into the twenty-second century. I was mesmerized by this incredible technological discovery.

I was pleased with how all the details of remote learning seemed to be falling smoothly into alignment upon the end of this first month of school. I felt that I had made significant progress toward acclimating to my new role. As I moved into October, I would experience several eye openers that would put my reality into perspective.

October Eye-Openers

(October 2021)

Surviving my first month felt like a major victory. Although prevailing through all of the September woes instilled a greater level of confidence in me, I knew that I was just seeing the tip of the iceberg. October was a month full of eye openers. Listening to a student bare his soul on camera, attending my first IEP meeting, learning of the blind spot that exists in remote learning, and ending the month with my first major Zoom bombing experience certainly altered many of my perspectives on teaching in a remote environment.

Our school counselor would join my Zoom typically one week out of every six weeks as one of our related arts rotations. She led social-emotional learning lessons and discussions with my class. At the beginning of October, it happened to be one of her rotations.

"Hey, loves! Who can tell me what month this is?" she asked the students. They raised their virtual hands, using a feature on Zoom. "Yes, ma'am?" she called on one of my students.

"Anti-bullying awareness month."

"Yes! That's correct! Anti-bullying awareness month!" replied the counselor. "So, today we're going to talk about kindness. What are some ways we can show kindness toward others?"

One student shared, "Giving compliments."

Another student volunteered, "Helping others when they need it."

However, a young man in my class decided to take this as an opportunity to bare his soul in front of everyone. "Yes, love?" the counselor asked him.

"So, my dad never knew what kindness was. He used to beat up my mom in front of me all the time. I would stand up for her and tell him that he needed to stop hitting her, kicking her, and punching her. Sometimes he would stop, but then sometimes he would get angrier and turn on me. He's hit me a bunch of times too. He knew that I was too little and not strong enough to fight back against him." My jaw was nearly on the floor, as he continued confessing the most intimate details of the paternal abuse from his father.

"We had to get the police involved, and they were at our house a lot. There was even an order against him where he wasn't allowed to come near us, and he couldn't see me without special permission. But, he actually died a few months ago so now I'll never see him again. I'm still trying to recover from the whole thing. That's why I have to go to therapy every week to talk about what happened and how I felt about it all. My therapist is really helping me get over the trauma and I like talking to her, because she's really good at listening and helping me cope with everything that happened."

I was in too much shock to say a word. The guidance counselor said, "Thank you so much for trusting us enough to share that, my friend. He definitely wasn't very kind to you or your mother, and he certainly was someone who needed to understand what anti-bullying month is." Afterwards, I spoke to the school counselor privately.

"Did he *really* just say all those things on camera?" I asked her in amazement.

"He sure did!" she replied.

"I can't believe he shared all that in front of the entire class! His poor mother would probably be absolutely humiliated if she knew he shared all of their family's personal business with everyone!" I exclaimed.

"But the fact he shared that is actually a good thing." the counselor explained. "I think it's great that he feels that he has a safe space in class to share something so personal." Her words led me to a powerful realization. The fact that this gentleman felt safe and comfortable enough to reveal such intimate details reflected my classroom management. I had succeeded in cultivating an environment where students felt safe and comfortable, and a strong sense of community had been established. As someone who tends to be very self-critical, I often fail to notice some of my own positive achievements until they are pointed out to me by someone else.

This student was not the only one who thrived in a safe online learning culture. Upon accepting the position as a virtual teacher, I had anticipated that the students who would struggle the most in a remote learning situation would be my students who received special education services. Like many others, I wondered, why their parents would not opt for them to attend in a face to face setting. I was concerned that these students would not be able to have their needs met in this type of learning format. However, it was in fact the contrary that proved to be true. This year, each of my students with IEPs have actually thrived in my class even more so than their non-disabled peers.

In October, I had my first student's IEP review meeting scheduled. This particular student is a testament as to how virtual learning can be a perfect fit for a student with a disability. Both of his parents logged onto Zoom to attend this meeting. We began reviewing his goals and areas of strength and weakness, and his mother and father began chiming in.

"This has been an excellent year for us, because of him." the student's mother said, referring to me. "He's been a blessing and a godsend for our son this year."

His father then began adding to his wife's remarks. "Yes! The last two years were extremely rough for our boy. He wasn't growing at all, and he was barely making any progress. Third and fourth grade were almost a wash for him. But this year, he's come so far! A lot of it has to do with you!" he exclaimed, pointing to me through the camera.

I began to blush. "Why, thank you! That means a lot to me."

"I'm serious!" the father continued. "His grades are higher, he feels way more confident, and he's not frustrated like he was in third and fourth grade."

"We hear him laughing and engaging with you when we're in the other room." his mother shared. "Whenever he's in a breakout room with his classmates, he's always participating. We don't have to worry about reminding him to log on Zoom and we never have to tell him it's time for class, he just jumps right on, because he really *wants* to be in your class!"

Flattered, I responded, "Wow! You guys, that really means a lot to me! Thank you so much! I'm so happy to know that I've been a positive part of his journey. Hearing your kind words really reminds me why I do what I do." Once the meeting was over and the couple logged off, the educational diagnostician, who was in charge of special education, and I took a few minutes to debrief and discuss the meeting we had just participated in.

"Wow! That was amazing!" she began. "They really seem to love you, and they're obviously very happy with how well he's doing in your class."

"I have noticed a lot of growth from him since the beginning of the year," I replied.

She nodded. "I think that's great. Maybe virtual academy was the perfect option for him this year."

"You know how many people have said to me this year, that virtual is the worst idea for a student with special education needs?" I remarked.

She shook her head. "That couldn't be farther from the truth." She then dived into another example of a student in my virtual class. "Look at that other friend in your class who was doing terribly last year when he was face to face. He was in the office constantly for behavior, he was disruptive in class, and he wasn't getting any of his classwork done. But this year he's *thriving* in virtual learning with you!"

"What do you think it is about the virtual environment that makes it better for these kids?" I asked her.

"I think a lot of it has to do with social pressures being removed." she explained. "For a lot of them, not having to deal with that extra social stress removes a big barrier; with that out of the way, they can really focus more on the academic part of school."

I then recalled a phone conversation with a parent that I had recently been part of. "It's so funny you say that, because I was actually just talking to a parent the other day and it's almost like what you just said was a confirmation of what she shared with me."

"Oh, who was it?" she asked.

I told her who the student was, and reminded her that he was also one of my students who had an IEP. "The mom told me that she feels like her son is doing a lot better in my class than he's ever done before. She said that, being remote, he doesn't feel like anyone notices his speech deficits and that his classmates aren't constantly watching him and noticing every time he struggles with something or makes a mistake. She also told me that being able to communicate through chat instead of verbally has been huge for him, because he doesn't have to feel nervous or worry about everyone hearing him stutter."

"And you know what, that's exactly why remote learning works for a lot of these kids!" my educational diagnostician agreed.

"But you know, there are still all the 'naysayers' who argue that remote learning needs to go away because kids can't learn proper social skills when they're not attending in person with others their own age." I explained.

She rolled her eyes and shook her head. "I hate it when people say that! Because, you know what, the whole purpose of the school system is to do one thing only: educate! That's it! It's not the job of the school system to socialize kids. As far as I'm concerned, parents can do that themselves. They can sign their kids up for sports, get them involved in social events outside of school, and arrange for them to get their social interaction plenty of other ways outside of school." I could not have agreed with this statement any more.

The removal of social pressures have allowed these students to release their inhibitions and overcome the obstacles that have deterred them for years. The stigma of being pulled to the infamous *back table* in a regular classroom was eliminated by private breakout rooms, where none of their peers even observe these students being pulled away for additional help. Eradicating the fear of judgment from classmates, has increased these students' confidence levels, which has in turn increased their grades and test scores. I have learned throughout my experiences with remote learning, that when a student feels safe and comfortable in the environment, they are all the more willing to take risks which yield great rewards.

Despite the fact that many students thrive in a virtual learning setting, I learned during this lengthy month of October that there is a reverse side to this as well. I call this a blind spot. One of the most dangerous virtual realities of remote learning, is having a blind spot. When I worked as a math tutor, years before I was a fully licensed teacher, I had filed a formal report with social services for a student whose father whipped him with a wet belt and left bruises on his body simply for earning a low grade in math. Instances of abuse and neglect, as well as serious problems on the home front often manifest themselves in ways that educators are trained to detect and report. In a virtual setting, these types of problems are far more easily concealed. I can attest to this from my own experience as a virtual teacher.

In the mix of my forty-two students, there was one in particular who stood out on my radar. It was a young lady, who I knew for a fact was very intelligent. My perception was that she was choosing to squander her gifts and talents by simply making poor choices. I was failing to consider any of the external factors she may have been facing in her home life, or elsewhere. In my young career as an educator, this was one mistake that still haunts me with guilt.

I noticed a chronic, recurring pattern with this student. On the rare occasions where she submitted work, which of course was seldom in a timely manner if she actually did, the quality was always impressive. Although the level of inconsistency I observed with her work completion sounded the alarm bell in my mind, her outstanding assignments were not my only cause of concern.

She was constantly logging in and out of Zoom, one of my greatest pet peeves. Often when she was logged on, her video was turned off and she was not visible. I perceived her as willfully ignoring my verbal cues and chat messages, where I constantly demanded that she strip off her virtual cloak of invisibility. After numerous promptings, I would finally deem her lack of response as an act of defiance and become frustrated with her.

My most frequent response to her unresponsiveness was to remove her from the Zoom meeting, and place her in the waiting room until she would agree to comply with my expectations. Although she would eventually return to the meeting and turn her camera on for short segments of class time, I saw minimal changes overall. She also began exhibiting an ongoing pattern of tardiness, habitually logging on late from lunch and recess. When I realized that my approach was failing to derive my desired results, I decided to reevaluate my tactics.

My next course of action was to reach out to the girl's mother, the single parent who possessed the sole responsibility of raising her. I sent multiple emails to the young lady's guardian during the first several weeks of school. Each of my emails provided detailed accounts of how her daughter was chronically late to class, how she was in danger of failing due to lack of work submission, and also how defiant she was for refusing to adhere to the expectations in my virtual classroom. For a long time, I received not a single word of correspondence and there were no replies to any of my messages. All I received were the occasional chats from the student, which I deemed to be nothing more than worthless excuses.

From time to time, the fifth grader would drop me a line stating that the reason she was not on Zoom was because her internet connection was unstable due to the fact that she was 'traveling'. Though I was not one to allow myself to be placated with excuses, I did observe that she was riding in a car during some of the few occasions that her camera was turned on. I was at the point of absolute frustration with this student, and the possibility that extenuating circumstances might be existing still did not occur to me.

Finally, after many unreturned phone calls and unread emails, I suddenly received a note from the girl's mother. I will never forget how it read: *I'm sorry that she has been missing so much time from class, and I know that there are times where she isn't on Zoom. We've been living in a homeless shelter downstate, and it's been hard for her to do virtual learning. We're trying to get her transferred to in-person learning.* At these words, I was overcome with sorrow and guilt.

A student who was already homeless and suffering from her family's circumstances of destitution and poverty had another weight on her shoulders to bear: me, her teacher. A person who should have been there for her to depend upon during this time of tribulation in her life, was instead someone inflicting further grief and pain upon her. My ignorance of her life's woes became one of my biggest regrets as a teacher.

Fortunately, although a request to switch from virtual to in-person learning seldom acquires approval in my district, a change of format was granted in this unique circumstance. This young lady was in the building within days of me receiving this communication from her mother. I realized that even though this student was likely uncertain of what the source of most of her meals would be, at minimum she was guaranteed one reliable meal per day in the school cafeteria. This still was insufficient to eradicate my feelings of guilt.

Each morning, I am forced to look this student in the eye as she passes me while I stand at my duty post. If I were her, I would want to avoid the insatiable Hitler who badgered me every day about my attendance and work completion, without taking a moment to consider what my circumstances were. Yet, my former pupil still approaches me daily with a warm smile, making a special point to speak to me and keep me informed of how her life was evolving. I am reminded every day of how easy it is to overlook the covert turmoil in the life of a student who is on the other side of a camera. I have been deeply impacted by this experience, and it has helped adjust my philosophy as an educator. Like many other thoughts of mine, it also keeps me awake some nights wondering how many other students could be silently suffering somewhere, off in the distance in a remote location that one may fail to ever realize.

October was approaching a close and I felt that I had already had a full year's worth of reality checks. The events of that month had given me a great deal to process. However, I was still in for one final adventure before the month of October was over. 28 October 2021 is still a very memorable day in my teaching career.

The term 'Zoom bombing' sounds hilarious and adorable. It is, unless of course you are the victim, and the hilarity is at your own expense. I failed to appreciate the humor when a group of Zoom bombers, although I will never know the exact number, decided to invade my meeting one afternoon.

There are three universal truths about all Zoom bombers. The first is that they are pathetic and have no ambition, which is why they cannot think of any better pastime other than intruding on a classroom that is not even their own. The second truth about Zoom bombers is that they all lack even the most basic literacy skills, which is obvious from the incoherent, misspelled, and grammatically incorrect chat messages they send. Finally, Zoom bombers have one primary objective: to cause the maximum amount of disruption possible. This is something that they were unfortunately very successful in achieving.

One Thursday after my students had finished their lunch and recess break, they began returning to my meeting for the rest of the day's instruction. As I was admitting my students back into the meeting, everything seemed normal. The number of participants was very close to what I typically have, and there were no unfamiliar names on the list whom I did not recognize.

Before I started my lesson, one of my students asked me, "Is it okay if I share a Kahoot game that I created? I'd love it if we could all play it together as a class, and you could play too." Since it was a brief multiple-choice game, it appealed to my students' interests, and I strive to make my students feel that their contributions are valued, I agreed to spare a few minutes of class time.

As with every Kahoot, every student is required to enter a nickname once they join with the game pin. All of a sudden, I noticed on my screen that someone had joined with the nickname *(my name) is fat*. My initial thought was that this was one of my students simply just teasing me. I just dismissed it with a chuckle, and a "very funny." I instructed the student who created the Kahoot to remove that user from the game, and I said, "Whoever that was, I need you to please join correctly with your first name *only*." A few moments later, the nickname *(my name) is ugly* appeared on the screen. At this point, I was growing upset. I view teaching as a position of being in service to my children, so I naturally took this personally.

I wanted to maintain my composure on camera, and I never wanted to lose my cool in the presence of my students. I had a strong rapport with my students, and I could not understand which of them would be doing this and why. So, still completely ignorant of my unauthorized guests, I decided that the best solution was for me to communicate openly with my students.

"Look," I began. "You guys are extremely valuable to me, and I do everything I can to make sure you feel safe and comfortable in my class. I care not only about your learning, but I care about you personally too. If any of you have an issue with me about something, I want you to know that it's okay to talk to me about it. I'll always listen and respect your feelings. Attacking me and calling me names doesn't solve the problem and it won't help me understand why you're feeling the way you are about me." I explained to them.

My students compassionately responded, "We would never say anything like that to you." There also were looks of widespread confusion on each of their faces.

My students could not make rhyme nor reason of what was taking place either. They knew that they were not the ones making those remarks, and they were also fairly certain that the vast majority of their classmates were not responsible either. For the next few minutes, there were no further disruptions and all was calm. Sadly, this brief period of peace and tranquility was short lived, however.

I continued my instruction, and I was reading aloud part of a text to my students. As I was reading, a public message visible to everyone appeared in the chatroom. *You're awesome and the best teacher ever,* the message read. I paused from my literature momentarily to acknowledge the flattering comment. As I returned to the material I was reading, another public message appeared in the chatroom. The sender's name was the same as the name of the sender of the first chat. The difference was, the tone of the second chat message abruptly changed. It read, *You're stupid, the worst teacher ever, and I hate your class.* I saw the wide eyed, jaw dropped expressions on all of my students' faces. My facial expression was similar to theirs. Initially, I could not even fathom how to address this comment.

Just then, the student spoke up and protested, "That's not me! I didn't write that rude chat! I swear! I wouldn't say something like that!"

I responded, "Okay, well if you didn't do it, who did? It's under your name."

"I think there must be someone else on Zoom under my name who's writing these things!" she suggested. *Hmm,* I thought. I pulled up my participant list. Surely enough, her claim was accurate.

I saw that there were participants with this exact same name, spelled identically, logged onto my Zoom meeting. I would easily have overlooked this, being a single teacher in a classroom with forty-two students to keep track of. I flipped through my grid views of my students, and I saw that the clone of this student had their video turned off. My first reaction was to ask this student to please turn on their camera. Not surprisingly, they balked at this polite request. It was then confirmed, that this individual was indeed an imposter.

Being the host of the Zoom meeting, I could just remove this intruder with a click of a button. That was the most logical way to squelch the disruptive outbursts, so I obviously took this step. I thought that the dilemma was finally resolved and that I could now resume where I left off in my lesson. I was about to discover that the joke was on me, and this was merely the beginning of the onslaught.

My students often encounter frequent connectivity issues

with their home internet, which is to be expected. This is the reason why many of my students may occasionally pop in and out of the Zoom meeting during class. On this unlucky Thursday afternoon, when I saw one of my students' names appear in the waiting room, I just admitted them to the meeting without giving any thought to it whatsoever. What I failed to realize was that on that fateful day, several imposters were exploiting this fact along with the fact that I had forty-two students in my class. Like insidious serpents, they slowly slithered into my class.

More public chat messages began rapidly appearing. Profanity began flying across the screens of everyone in my meeting. Sadly though, these illiterate attention seekers could not even manage to spell the words 'ass' or 'suck' correctly. Even a six or seven-year-old could have done better than these losers. Although, I must applaud the originality of their next trick.

Apparently, while I had myself in a spotlighted view for the students during the time I was reading to them, our unwelcomed guests had taken pictures and screenshots of my face, unbeknownst to me. They decided to change their Zoom background screens to the picture of my face which they had discreetly obtained. To add to their display, they each renamed themselves 'Eat My Ass'. They made sure to post a caption of this on the background picture as well, to ensure that none of my students would miss their vulgar and obnoxious gesture. This did not evade my students' detection. Additionally, it did not manage to fly beneath the radar of the parents and guardians who were home with my remote learners as well.

Within seconds later, I could see adults approaching their children from behind and sticking their faces into the camera. I could see my students conversing with their guardians and pointing at their screens, which I could infer was them pointing out the lovely chat messages, captions, and photos of my smiling face. I could see looks of confusion and disgust on the faces of these people. My phone and email began flooding with emails and texts from parents. They were quite curious as to what was occurring and who was responsible for the inappropriate comments. Above all, they were understandably displeased that their children were witnessing these remarks and that their learning was being disrupted. Just when I thought that the situation could not become any more uncomfortable for me, I was proved incorrect.

As the level of profanity doubled and the obnoxious onslaught escalated, I heard a knock at my classroom door. Through the glass, I could distinguish a familiar face. It was none other than the elementary assistant superintendent for the school district. She entered the room with a beaming smile on her face. "I'm here to pop in and observe your class to get a feel for how virtual learning is going," she said.

My face turned red and I began to feel light headed. *Perfect timing,* I thought to myself. In the midst of a crisis, a panicked response flew off of my lips. "I'm being Zoom bombed!" I frantically shouted. "They're cursing in the chat and getting everyone upset! I need help, right now!" She stepped behind my monitor to confirm for herself what was taking place. After viewing a few of the vulgar chat messages, she looked at me and nodded.

"I'm going to get help right now," she assured me. A few minutes later, she returned with the geek squad and my assistant principal.

I was instructed by all three of them to assign my students an asynchronous task and end the meeting for the next half hour, in order to afford us the opportunity to investigate and correct the problem. I told my class, "Guys, read a book on Amplify and come back in half an hour." And then I abruptly ended the Zoom meeting, cutting off some of my students, mid-sentence. The rest of the afternoon was a whirlwind.

The number of parent inquiries soared through the ceiling. I could not the blame them for being alarmed. On the other hand, communication needed to be handled with caution. "The last thing we want them thinking is that we don't have control," my assistant principal explained. So, while the geek squad devised a solution, she helped me craft a narrative to calm down the families and assure them that everything was fine, although I felt like quitting that day.

Meanwhile, the geek squad pulled the Zoom report with the list of all meeting logins for the day, along with any email addresses that participants used to log on. Unfortunately, we were outsmarted by the Zoom bombers who used no traceable email addresses. We could not apprehend the culprits, and we could also not shut class down for the remainder of the day. So, birth was given to a temporary solution that would live in infamy among my students henceforth: Zoom lockdown mode.

I felt this was the most appropriate for our quick fix. I figured that since face to face students got to partake in lockdown drills whenever an unsafe situation presents itself, my virtual students should not be excluded. To be able to safely continue instruction with my students for the last hour of the school day without Zoom bombers interfering, I revoked every student's ability to unmute themselves and I limited the chatroom to where students could only message me directly. The screenshare feature was disabled as well. The direct messages I received from my students in the chatroom were a clear indicator that Zoom lockdown mode was not a popular move; however, it also kept bedlam at bay.

At the end of the school day, the geek squad ingeniously ensured that I would never again suffer humiliation by Zoom bombers. He taught me how to authenticate my Zoom settings, meaning that from that day on, students could only log into my Zoom meeting with a valid district Google account. This would strip any Zoom bombers of their cloak of invisibility once and for all. The geek squad was also thorough enough to create a helpful video explaining how to log on in this new way step by step, which roughly one-fifth of my families did not even bother to take the time to watch. This day will continue to remain unforgotten by my students.

Conveniently, there was a faculty meeting scheduled after school that day. At the end, my vice-principal instructed all virtual teachers to stay behind. She and the geek squad met with each of us. "So, guys, we just want to be proactive. There was an incident in fifth-grade today with intruders in Zoom, and we want to make sure this doesn't happen to anyone again," my assistant principal explained. "To prevent this from happening again, we need each of you to authenticate your Zoom settings."

The geek squad chimed in. "If you are unsure how to do that, here are the steps," he said, pointing to a sheet of instructions he handed out to each of us. "Tonight, you'll need to update your Zoom links and send the new link out to your families in an email. I'm also going to create a video that explains to parents how to help their kids log in with their district Google account." After the meeting, I stayed behind for a moment to debrief with my assistant principal.

"That was horrible, what happened today." I exclaimed. "Go figure, shit just had to go down right when the assistant superintendent would waltz in to observe my class."

She laughed and replied, "It's never a good time to get Zoom bombed. I have to say though, I'm glad she got to witness that. She needs to see for herself the struggles we have in virtual academy, and what we deal with every day."

I was inclined to agree. Despite the many sentiments within the district that the task of being a virtual teacher was somehow easier and less stressful, there are many stressful aspects of teaching online. This was but one of many eye openers that I had experienced during this long month of October.

Following the Zoom bombing incident, nearly every time we played a game of Kahoot, I had at least one student who would still revisit that fateful afternoon. Above all, my students remember this day as the day which gave birth to the bane of their existence. I still snicker when I see the look of dread on my students' face whenever they hear the threat of Zoom lockdown mode emanating from my lips.

Fortunately, November would be a shorter month with Veterans Day, parent conferences, and Thanksgiving break. Although a shorter month is never a guarantee of less excitement, it at least ensures more time to breathe and process all the challenges that come.

November Adventures

(November 2021)

I was grateful to finally be into the month of November. With the first two months of school under my belt, I was beginning to feel a sense of relief. Although teaching in a remote setting never gets easier, each challenge makes me stronger. That month, albeit short, was most definitely not boring. Getting to be part of my students' journey of receiving information about puberty, having conflict with a momzilla come fully to a head, and witnessing sheer heartbreak were definitely in the cards for me in the coming days in November.

Being a fifth-grade teacher means that my students are in that special year when it is time for them to hear 'the speech'. For one-hour per day for an entire week, our district invites an external presenter to provide each fifth-grade class with information and insight into how their bodies would be developing, some of the physical changes they would be undergoing, and why it was normal for them to experience certain sensations, thoughts, and urges.

My district works with the Adolescent Resource Center (A.R.C.). During my tenure as a long-term substitute in fifth grade the year prior, I was sitting in a team Zoom meeting when the other teachers made a reference to 'A.R.C. class.' I was the only male teacher on the team, and I had absolutely no clue what 'A.R.C. class' was. So, I naively chimed in and inquired of my female colleagues, "Pardon me for asking, but what is A.R.C.? I've never heard that acronym before."

Each of the women immediately roared with laughter. Naturally, they began teasing me and making remarks such as, "Oh, you'll get to learn lots of neat stuff."

One of the paraprofessionals teased, "Oh, this is a probably a step down for him. I guarantee, he's heard worse from T and V over in third grade." They all cracked up at this remark as well.

I regretted unmuting myself and opening my mouth. This inspired a very amusing conversation, at least they believed it was. I especially wished I had remained silent when one of my female teammates whose husband was a chiropractor shared with the group, "My husband ought to come sit through A.R.C. too. He hasn't adjusted me in a month, because he's always too tired when he gets home." This inspired me to reach for the stop video button on Zoom and switch my camera off. Of course, this did not go unnoticed.

"Aww, I think we're making the poor guy uncomfortable," they all joked. Needless to say, I never forgot what A.R.C. was and I remembered exactly what to expect each year as a fifth-grade teacher.

Despite the fact that all my students were virtual, the A.R.C. presenter still needed to work from my classroom. The solution to my Zoom bomber problem meant that she could not enter my Zoom meeting since she did not have a district email address or Google account. This meant I would be treated to a front row seat.

I distributed an email to parents a week prior to the start date of the presentation, informing them of their legal rights to opt their children out of these sessions at their discretion. A few of the families expressed their wishes to address the more delicate topics with their children themselves. One parent, who was the only person I knew of in the year 2021 who still refused to have an email account, was blindsided when that week of information came around.

During the first day of the presentation, I was called down to the front office by the secretary. "I just got off the phone with a parent. She called in and was raising a holy fit. She was going on about how it was totally outrageous and unacceptable that her daughter was exposed to such inappropriate content, and how she was utterly offended as a parent that her little girl had to be subjected to all that," explained the secretary. The parent who called in the complaint turned out to be none other than the misandrist.

I immediately tracked down my assistant principal. "We just got an angry parent phone call about A.R.C.," I told her, breathing heavily. "She's pissed off to the hills that her innocent little girl was exposed to information about her reproductive organs."

"Didn't you let the parents know in advance that the A.R.C. presenter was coming in this week?" she inquired.

"Yes!" I replied. "I sent a mass email out to all of my families a whole *week* in advance about this, and I gave them the opt out form if they didn't want their kids participating. I even mentioned that they could still opt out during A.R.C. week, if they decided they were uncomfortable with any of it. But this asshole is one of the only parents in the 21st century that refuses to get an email account. We've offered multiple times to set one up for her but she keeps resisting! So, the dingbat probably didn't receive the notice."

My assistant principal laughed and shrugged. "That's on her, don't sweat it," she said to me. So, I pushed it out of my mind and pressed onward.

There were major advantages to providing students this type of information in a virtual setting. I was able to ensure that my class felt safe and comfortable throughout the entirety of the presentation, by initiating Zoom lockdown mode. I disabled students' ability to unmute themselves or post insensitive or inappropriate comments in the chatroom for their classmates to view. Any student who wanted to inquire about any of the information the presenter shared could only send a private message to either myself or the presenter. Judging by the reactions I noticed from my students, I doubt they would have felt comfortable speaking out loud anyway.

When the presenter began talking about erections, ejaculation and wet dreams, I noticed about three-fourths of my students' videos switch off. They felt too awkward and embarrassed to even show their faces on camera. Normally I am very firm about my expectation of cameras being on at all times, but this was a time when I made a necessary exception. I received a couple of interesting private chats. One of my gentlemen had a question about size and wanted to know how big *it* could get. I heard from some of the families about how fascinated their children were with the information they received.

After the week of information was over, I spoke to one mom who shared with me that her fifth-grader asked her, "Did I just learn about making babies?" She also had an adult son who sat through this same presentation when he was the same age. The mom shared with me how she 'wanted to fall through the floor' when her eldest son came from school and told her 'I know why my pee pee hurts sometimes now'. I still recollect details from my fifth-grade puberty information class.

When I was still a student, long before our new virtual

reality, there was no opportunity for my classmates and I to send a private chat message when we had questions. We were given small slips of paper to write our questions on, and the two school nurses read them aloud to the class and answered them. I remember wanting to leave the room because my classmates could not resist making their immature remarks and laughing at the top of their lungs, refusing to show any respect for others.

One of the students in my class had immaturely asked the presenter, 'Can two fags have babies?' at which my entire class roared with laughter. Another student, one of the class clowns in my grade, boldly asked, 'Is butt sex any good?' Then, there was a classmate of mine who thought it would be hilarious to assert, "Oh yeah, now that we've learned about what PMS is, we know why all girls are so awful for a week every month." I wish Zoom lockdown mode had existed back then.

I was certainly glad that my fifth-graders had a much better experience than I had at their age. My memory of my own puberty seminar motivated me to prevent any of my students from feeling as uncomfortable as I had felt during my fifth-grade year. I am very fortunate to have such a mature and respectful group of learners in my virtual class, and that week reminded me of this.

Although having to deal with A.R.C. class was a bit awkward and uncomfortable for me as an educator, I would choose A.R.C. any day over having to contend with a vicious momzilla. Unfortunately, we do not have the privilege of choosing who our students or parents are in the field of public education.

At times, communicating with parents and guardians can be an onerous duty. Almost every family that I communicate with is highly receptive, respectful, and very involved in their child's education. However, regardless of geographical location, the inevitable fact is that there will always be a small number of those special parents who are every teacher's worst nightmare. Being in a remote setting does not change this. I had one student whose mother greatly contributed to my already high stress level as a first-year teacher.

The level of apathy this particular student had demonstrated since the start of the school year had been alarming. Her favorite avoidance tactic was logging in and out of Zoom constantly. She also did not believe that the requirement to attend full days of remote school like her classmates was a standard that should be applicable to her. The amount of instructional time that she missed during the first few months of school was absurd. In conjunction with her refusal to attend, this young lady also felt that she was entitled to simply achieve passing grades and automatically be promoted onto the next grade level without submitting a single assignment. She had more than twenty combined outstanding assignments by the time Halloween rolled around. To gain insight into how she developed this attitude, I had to look no further than her mother.

After more than a month of school and having received hardly any work from this student, I contacted her mother to make her aware of the situation. My hope and my assumption was that this woman would be concerned over the fact that more than half of the first marking term had ended and her daughter had already fallen so far behind. Much to the contrary, I received only a single line of correspondence. Momzilla's short reply consisted of: *We all had coronavirus and things have been hectic.* Despite my gut feeling that this excuse was most likely a fabricated lie, I sent a courteous reply offering my sympathies and wishing everyone in the household well. Several more weeks of school elapsed, and I still saw absolutely no improvement in this pattern of behavior.

As a matter of fact, this girl's attendance became more inconsistent and she was still refusing to complete any of her work. I knew that this meant the need for follow-up with Momzilla. My next email to Momzilla included a list of all the outstanding assignments. It was obvious the Momzilla was both shocked and annoyed with me, yet still unconcerned with her daughter's success in school. This was the turning point where I began noticing the increasing level of hostility from Momzilla.

A few days later, I was confronted by the hostile Momzilla. "I want to know why you would mark my daughter absent for just one minute or so late!" she demanded. "That's insane! It doesn't make any sense to mark her absent for that," she insisted. These comments from Momzilla brought my blood to a roaring boil. Her daughter had definitely been missing large quantities of time on a regular basis which greatly exceeded one or two minutes, but I was not about to begin an argument and exchange blows with this woman.

I decided it was time for matters to be taken to the next level. I replied, "You know, I think it would probably be a good idea for us to set up a conference with the administration. I'll reach out to them and we can go ahead and set up a date for that." Judging from her radio silence afterwards, Momzilla clearly was not a proponent of my idea. I was not about to just forget about all that had transpired and let Momzilla off that easily.

My principal and I scheduled a time to meet with Momzilla on Zoom. She agreed in writing and accepted the time we offered. When her date came up, I was prepared with all of my data and documentation, and my principal was ready to address the concerns with me as well. My principal and I waited more than fifteen minutes for Momzilla to log on and join us for the conference. "I don't think she's coming," my principal concluded.

"I can't believe she stood us up!" I remarked. "Is it strictly apathy, or she is just too much of a coward to face us?"

My principal shrugged her shoulders. "Honestly, I'm not sure. But, we're going to get the message through to her either way," she assured me. There was not even the common courtesy of a cancellation notice, not that we would expect such from this woman of course. It was clear that Momzilla had no desire to cooperate with us for the sake of her daughter's learning.

As a result, the verdict at report card time was quite inauspicious. The young fifth grader received failing grades in all subjects, the number of days tardy and absences listed on her report card were higher than the number of days present, and her specific competency marks for each subject area reflected a need for improvement. Instead of Momzilla recognizing her daughter's first report card as a sign that her parental intervention was necessary, she dismissed it. It was easier for her to use me a scapegoat as opposed to making an adjustment to her laissez faire style of parenting.

The number of missing assignments and lost instructional time continued to accumulate. One day, her daughter logged out of Zoom for an entire hour and then returned moments before lunch and recess were about to begin. I pulled the fifth grader into a breakout room to remind her of the expectations and that she would be held accountable for what she had missed. Later that day, I received another one of Momzilla's ever so congenial emails. This one read, *Her tablet died. The charger is not charging the way it is supposed to. She left it plugged in all night and it's still not charging fully. You should be more understanding or at least ask if she is having problems or issues before giving her attitude about what you think she's doing here at home, when she is dealing with the Wi-Fi connection and her tablet.* I had to close the lid to my laptop and step away for a breather. I absolutely refused to indulge a parent communication like this one. This email did not even deserve my response, so I did not bother to reply. *I'll just forward it on,* I decided. My refusal to dignify Momzilla's infantile behavior further fueled her contempt for me.

Keeping Zoom bombers out of my class was easy. Keeping out an indignant parent was much trickier. As I was leading a whole group lesson one afternoon, Momzilla came behind her daughter's screen and unmuted herself while I was in the middle of teaching. She interrupted me mid-sentence and announced who she was. "Please don't interrupt my class while I'm in the middle of teaching," I cut her off. However, she continued, "I need to talk to you for a minute – now." Normally, I would have muted her or removed her daughter from my Zoom meeting. However, since I was sharing my screen and I was just flustered from the encounter, I did not think to reach for any of those buttons. Finally, she ended with, "I'm taking my daughter off for the day. We're gonna go to the hospital now." I knew that this was another bold-faced lie, but I was just grateful when Momzilla finally decided to shut-up. Although she did not threaten me, curse at me, or scream at me in front of my class, I was livid over the mere fact that she had the audacity to continue disrupting my class after I made it clear that was what she was doing. *She couldn't just have the decency to send me an email or private chat message,* I concluded. A few minutes later, my classroom phone rang.

It was our virtual academy registrar. Our post marking

period parent conference week was approaching soon, where there was no school for students in order to provide every family with the opportunity to sign up for a meeting slot with their child's teacher. "I have a parent in my ear right now demanding your sign-up link for conferences next week," the registrar explained. Without even asking, I instinctively knew who it was. When my principal learned of the events that transpired that afternoon, she decided that enough was enough.

My principal was extremely methodical in her next approach. Like me, she could not make logical sense of why Momzilla was demanding a conference with me when she did not even attend the previous one she was offered. Nonetheless, she was ready to handle Momzilla.

My principal has a natural gift for dealing with contentious parents, and sending a firm message that resonates with them while simultaneously respecting their feelings and dignity. So, she decided to craft an email to Momzilla. This email was absolutely brilliant, and I could not have surpassed the level of tactfulness myself.

My fearless leader reminded her of the fact that she stood both of us up for our last conference, but if she wanted to reschedule another, she was welcome to do so. I also loved the last line of her email, cleverly but gently letting Momzilla know that her daughter might not be promoted to sixth grade next year if her antics continued. We still held out hope that Momzilla would finally show her face for a conference.

Parent conference week was approaching quickly. I continued maintaining my civil line of communication with Momzilla, practically begging her to attend a conference with us. Momzilla agreed to another date and time for a Zoom meeting. The time came, and my principal and I patiently awaited her login. Once again, the outcome was the same. Momzilla was a no show, yet again. Predictably, her daughter's mentality remained unchanged as well, along with her grades, attendance, and effort.

The contentious encounters with Momzilla and the unwavering apathy of her daughter provided me with a vital reality check. It was always my feeling that I was solely responsible for the success of every student and that their failure was a reflection on me as a teacher. I learned from Momzilla and her daughter that this is not always true. I have to remind myself that I am not responsible for the drowning victim who rejects my life raft and swats away my hand which tries to rescue them. Also, I vowed no longer to take Momzilla's jabs personally and let them ruin another day for me. Afterall, like the realist in me always tells people: it is impossible to make chicken salad from chicken shit.

What truly sickens me to my core is how remiss parents like these manage to retain custody of their children, while caring guardians who genuinely love their children have terrible experiences. Any educator who believes that they possess the ability to forecast what each day might offer is either naïve or self-deceived. Just when I was beginning to feel as though I had already witnessed my share of flabbergasting events in this field, my jaw was jolted to the ground once again. I can recall no college professor nor mentor who shared such a unique experience as one I encountered in the fall of 2021.

A few months into the school year, I had a new student enroll in my class. She had a younger sibling who'd enrolled in a lower grade within our virtual academy as well. They were both being raised by their grandmother, whom I have become well acquainted with. She also enlightened me regarding their family situation as well as its impact on the girls.

The girls' grandmother arranged a conference with me in November to explain the situation. "The state appointed me their legal guardian. Their biological mother's drug abuse habits got them taken away from her, and the state asked me to step up and take them in. I love my grandbabies, and I had no choice because there was no way I was going to turn my back on them. I'm raising these girls right now as my own. It's not easy doing this while I'm holding a demanding full-time job that makes me commute across state lines every single day."

I was overwhelmed with empathy for her. "How do you manage to juggle all this responsibility?" I asked in awe.

"I do whatever I have to do. I also have to employ a babysitter for the children during weekdays while I'm at work. I have to trust this person to make sure that both of my girls are logging on, doing their work, and engaging in remote learning like they're supposed to. Sometimes, I'm not sure how good she is at doing that," she explained.

To claim that the babysitter was derelict in her duty, would be a mild understatement. As a result of constantly logging in late and engaging in off-task behaviors due to lack of supervision, the fifth-grade student's performance in my class showed a decline. I reached out to the grandmother to let her know what was happening.

As she answered the phone, I began, "I'm calling to touch base about your granddaughter's attendance. She's been coming into my Zoom meeting almost an hour late each morning, and I've been noticing also that she's been making a habit of logging back on from lunch and recess about half an hour late as well."

"Ugh!" reacted the woman. "I've told their sitter she needs to be checking on and them and making sure they're logged on when they're supposed to be! I'm going to have to have a talk with her! Thanks for letting me know."

In the coming days, I noticed an improvement in the girl's attendance and work completion. I was not in doubt that the grandmother truly loved and cared for her granddaughters. Then, one day the fifth-grader did not show up to my Zoom. I later received a disturbing email from the grandmother, which prompted me to call her immediately.

"So, I had to fire the girls' babysitter today," she explained to me. "She decided to take both of my girls to the pharmacy to get vaccinated for COVID-19 without even telling me. When I came home from work last night, I found out from them what she did. I told this woman that she had absolutely no right to make any kind of health decision for my granddaughters without consulting me first. So, I fired her and told her she was never coming near my grandbabies ever again. On her way out, she took—no—she *stole* all of their technology on her way out. She took their school laptops, their school iPads, and their chargers. She took everything! Until we get it all back, they're not going to be able to log onto Zoom or do any of their work."

I was absolutely livid. "She did what?" I said in disbelief. "Oh, hell no! I'd charge her for that! That's crazy! She had absolutely no legal right to do that to your grandchildren! Who does that woman think she is? And why did she take their technology?"

The grandmother replied, "Oh she just took it to be spiteful. On her way out, she told me 'I've done more for these girls than you ever have. You're not just going to take them from me.' And so, she's holding their devices hostage."

"How dare she!" I asserted. "I'm going to talk to the principal about this ASAP – but I'm pretty sure she's actually committed prosecutable theft by taking those devices from them.

Plus, those are school property." I followed up with my principal and forwarded all of the information from the grandmother on to her.

The grandmother and the principal communicated, and the grandmother agreed to press charges against the sitter. She went to her local precinct, where she was coldly greeted by a grouchy desk sergeant.

"What do you need?" he mumbled, not even glancing up from his computer.

"I need to file a report against my former baby sitter who stole all of my granddaughters' technology. Can you tell me what paperwork I need to fill out?" The officer rolled his eyes.

"You don't fill out paperwork. Go to the sitter's house, wait outside in your car, and call for a police officer. They'll dispatch someone to meet you there, and they'll approach her with you to ask for the stolen technology."

The grandmother did as instructed. She parked her vehicle outside the woman's house with peeling paint and damaged siding and waited over forty-five minutes for a police officer to arrive. The neighborhood felt completely unsafe to her. Graffiti covered the nearby street signs, fences surrounded each home, and a crime watch sign was visible from her window. Finally, she started her car and drove away, realizing that she had been stood up by the authorities.

Frustrated with the police, the grandmother resorted to a new course of action. She decided to obtain a court order that would force the sitter to relinquish the stolen technology. The court granted the order and the girls' persistent guardian believed that the end to this headache was directly over the horizon. On the other hand, the manipulative former helper saw this as a golden opportunity to strike.

In response to the court order, she falsely claimed that the girls' legal guardian was neglecting both children and that she had been forced to assume the role of their primary caretaker. Her claims were forwarded on to the department of family services, who deemed it fit to initiate an inquisition.

The guardian worked a high paying job which required her to commute out of state. She refused to take a job closer to home to avoid sacrificing the level of financial stability that her current occupation allowed her to provide for her granddaughters. Much to her detriment, this came under scrutiny by the child services representative. "God forbid there's ever an emergency, you'll be too far away to get home to these children," the representative told her. The representative continued, "From my standpoint, it looks like since the babysitter had to do the responsible thing and take both of your grandchildren to receive their coronavirus vaccinations, this shows evidence to corroborate the sitter's claims that you've clearly been derelict in your duties as a legal guardian."

Therefore, she was stripped of custody of her granddaughters. Devastated by the outcome, her heart bled. Having fought for five years to keep these girls out of the very system that they were about to be remanded into once again, she was in utter disbelief over this outcome. As an educator, I was deeply affected by what these children and their grandmother endured.

Both of these children had already been encountering serious academic struggles, due to already being relocated multiple times. Another move would be even more harmful to them, and might even cause them to rebel in their next educational placement. As a young man, I had a very rigid, black and white outlook on all situations in life. It used to be my belief that if offered the right to a free public education, everyone should thrive and be successful no matter what. Working in this field has brought me to the epiphany that some of my earlier beliefs were fallacious. Through examples such as these, I have learned that empathy and compassion are the cornerstones in relating to people from all walks of life. During the course of the pandemic, I feel that many of us have come to forget our understanding of empathy and compassion due to isolation from others. However, the significance of these qualities will never dwindle nor dissipate as long as we are all human beings living on this earth.

As Thanksgiving break approached, I realized that I had much to be thankful for. I enjoyed making a positive difference in the lives of my students, and it is a gift that I have been fortunate enough to be able to give. Many parents also appreciated my efforts as well, which is one of my true rewards of teaching.

At the end of November, I received one of the kindest parent emails of my young career. It read, *I appreciate all of your patience, communication, and kindness. I never experienced a teacher as kind, patient, and dependable as you.* The parent also submitted a copy of this email to my administration and to human resources as well. This email brought me to tears, and it continues to serve as my reminder of why I entered the profession.

I was grateful to have a break, and I knew that with only a few short weeks in the month of December, winter break would not evade me for long. However, I was about to discover a December surprise that was awaiting me.

Class

(December 2021)

Finally, the of month December had come upon me and winter break was looming directly over the horizon. Although I was still completely overwhelmed and had only four months under my belt as a teacher, I was beginning to feel as though each day was running more smoothly. I felt as though, at last, I was getting into a good rhythm and that I was starting to get a grasp on my job. However, the reality of being a teacher is that once you begin to feel comfortable, there is always an abrupt change that jerks you forward in your seat. I was about to experience one of these changes.

I had finally adjusted and become familiar with nearly every feature that Zoom had to offer. I was now used to this platform and fully comfortable with it. In the middle of December, the virtual team was summoned for a meeting one afternoon. It was led by the geek squad who had something important to reveal to the virtual team.

"So guys, we're thinking about moving away from Zoom for the rest of this year." he announced. My heart sank and I felt as though I had been socked in the gut. "We've been investigating a platform called Class for the past couple months. You guys probably remember a couple months ago when the company did their remote presentation for us… Well, we've decided we're going to experiment with it and see if it's a direction we should move in as a virtual academy." I was in full blown panic mode. I was not prepared to transition to an entirely new platform, mid-year.

The geek squad continued explaining away the intriguing features of this new platform. "So, Class offers a lot of cool features that we can't get through Zoom. With Class, you can actually make a seating chart. One of the biggest problems we have with Zoom right now is that kids' faces are always shifting around. They're moving around constantly on the screen, and you can barely keep track of the ones you're trying to talk to. But with Class, you will actually be able to position students so that they appear on the first page, at the top of your screen so you can monitor them closely without having to flip through multiple pages." As I looked around the room, I noticed many of my colleagues smiling and nodding in approval.

"I believe a couple months ago, the presenters said it was supposed to help with engagement too, correct?" I asked.

The geek squad nodded. "Yes. Class also has this neat feature which actually tracks the amount of talk time for each student every day. It will automatically generate a report with the number of minutes that each student spends talking. And you'll be able to watch every breakout room at the same time and see who's participating and who's not. It won't be like Zoom where you have to bounce from room to room to check on each group one at a time." During my first post-observation conference at the beginning of December, my assistant principal pointed out breakout room participation as an area for potential growth with my level of student engagement. I figured this might be a solution.

The geek squad continued raving about all the amazing features that Class had to offer. "Every day, it even puts kids into color categories based on their participation. You don't have to worry about trying to keep track of the kids' attendance minutes either when they're logging in and out constantly, because Class will do that for you too."

This, I was very relieved to hear. "So, this means I won't have to spend my free time pulling Zoom reports any more and trying to document the number of minutes that my sneaky higher fliers creep out!" I exclaimed excitedly.

"That's right!" geek squad replied.

So far, Class was sounding awesome. I was almost excited to embrace this new experimental platform. There was still just one lingering concern that I had, which was safety and security.

"Now, I have to ask: does Class have a feature where I can require authentication for students to join where they have to be logged into their district Google accounts?" I inquired.

Geek squad hesitated for a moment, then responded, "Well, that's the one downside right now. We can't authenticate with Class like we can with Zoom. That's a kink we're still in the process of working out. And there's another thing you'll have to verify and approve each student individually as they enter. Unfortunately, you can't let them all in at once like you can on Zoom. Getting them all in the first time is probably going to take a while." I was now beginning to feel more apprehensive about the possible transition to the new platform.

"So, when do we have to be fully transitioned from Zoom to Class?" I asked geek squad.

"Well," he said, "right now, there isn't a firm roll out date. It's just in the experimental phase, and we kind of want to test it first and see how it goes. But, we're asking everyone to try it with their class after we come back from winter break. Then, we'll see how it goes, we'll get a feel for how it works, and then we'll go from there."

With five months of school remaining, I wondered how this new platform would pan out. Regardless, I was sure of one inevitable truth: there were many adventures that lay ahead in the coming months between winter break and summer vacation. I would be in for many more trials, tribulations, successes, failures, eye openers, and surprises.

The Never-Ending Struggle

Unlike the stench of cow manure, which gradually dissipates, the trials and tribulations of teaching, whether virtually or in any other setting, never dwindles. Part of the reality of working in a field where professional growth is ongoing, is that the growing pains run parallel. Even surviving my practicum experiences, several long-term positions, and the first five months of my first official year of teaching on the books has failed to alleviate my stress level, nor has it allowed me to experience any feeling of finally becoming acclimated.

Despite the fact that I refused to heed my mom's words of wisdom coming from decades of experience, I finally had to acknowledge that she made several valid points. In the few days leading up to winter break, I was forced to admit to her the accuracy of her forewarnings.

"So you're almost halfway through your first year!" she exclaimed.

"Yeah," I replied, and nodded unenthusiastically.

"How do you feel?" she asked.

I let out a deep sigh and shook my head. "You know, I've got to be honest, you were right about a lot of things. I had no idea what I was really getting into."

She nodded her head and smiled. "I told you so." Having fought this woman tooth and nail in the process of changing my major from actuarial science to teaching, I was extremely reluctant to give her the satisfaction of validation.

"Haha, yeah, bet it feels good to be right, huh?"

Her expression changed to a sympathetic one. "No, that's not it at all. I want you to be happy! I want you to enjoy what you're doing! It's just that you're my son, and I know you; you get stressed very easily. I know how anxious you get; I just don't want to see this job take a toll on you. Trust me, for someone like you who worries a lot, this job is very taxing," she explained.

Of course, my mother was once again correct. As a very high-strung person with an anxiety level higher than most, this high-stress, high-demand field has already proven to lack compatibility with my personality. The day before winter break, my emotions had finally reached a point where they were ready to erupt like a raging volcano.

Response To Intervention (RTI), which is a layered approach to providing additional support for students with learning needs early on, is something that I lacked a thorough understanding of upon entering into this full-time role. The number of additional minutes of support and services that I provided to specific students had to be documented in a specific way electronically. Additionally, there is a process where we are required to make recommendations to either release students from receiving the extra support, continue providing them same amount and type of support they receive, or refer them for additional support. I failed to not only document the amount of weekly minutes in the system that I provided each of these students with, but I also forgot to complete my recommendations. This oversight was quickly brought to my attention by the instructional coach.

In effort to salvage the situation and minimize the impact that my mistake would have, I scurried down to my principal's office within two hours of realizing my mistake. I knocked on her door, with my heart pounding in my chest and a lump in my throat. She looked from her computer and smiled when she saw my figure standing in the doorway. "Hey there! What's up? Come on in!" she greeted me, gesturing for me to have a seat on her couch. "So, what's going on today?" she asked, with a look of curiosity on her face.

I took a deep breath, and paused for a moment. Finally, I began, "Look, I just think I should come out and say it: I fucked up, I'm here to own my mistake and face the music," I replied.

A now even more puzzled expression showed on her face, as she was squinting her eyes. "O-okay? Well, what happened?"

"I didn't enter in my RTI minutes," the words frantically poured out of me. "I didn't put in my recommendations for RTI either. It was a mistake! I swear, I had no clue! I've never had to do this before, and with all I've had on my plate to remember and with forty-two kids in my class—it—I don't know. It just fell through the cracks like a fog, I guess."

My principal nodded her head, hesitated for a moment as she thought carefully. She began, "Okay, that's something I would just assume that you'd know, but I do understand that you're a new teacher, and I know you've had a lot to keep track of this year. The good news is this isn't the end of the world. I mean, it could delay the process for some kids getting more help but last time I checked, there aren't any RTI police. If there are, I certainly haven't met them."

I sighed in relief, and chuckled lightly. "Wow! Thank you for being so understanding about this."

"You're going to make mistakes," she replied. "You're new. You learn and grow from them. You didn't know about the RTI thing before, but now you do. And honestly that's partly on us too. We sometimes just assume everybody's good and knows exactly what to do, but maybe we should've checked up on you to see if you needed any clarification. But in the future, please ask if you don't know something."

I nodded and agreed. "I feel like there's a lot I don't know. There's so much shit to keep track of, I feel like I'm constantly trying to play whac-a-mole. I just am starting to feel like I can't do anything right and that I completely suck at my job," I explained.

My principal shook her head. "You've been here less than six months… of course you haven't mastered your job yet! No first-year teacher has! Don't expect next year to be much different either," she exclaimed.

"The stress might kill me before I even make it to next year," I responded.

"You've got to rein that in," she retorted. "Truthfully, most of your anxiety is self-inflicted; we're not putting the pressure on you. You're heaping it all on yourself. Every new teacher is so worried about getting in trouble for not knowing something, or for looking stupid when they're struggling, when the reality is: we *want* you guys to ask us questions! We *expect* that you're going to struggle and have areas that you need to grow in. You really need to lower that wall that you have up, and just stop beating yourself up and worrying about every little thing. Some of the stuff you worry about is petty – don't sweat the small stuff!"

I have to admit that my principal knows me well, and her comments were true. Finding a way to de-stress in such a highly stressful field is a seemingly impossible mission for me to accomplish. The fact that I am constantly dodging quicksand traps at every turn in this job, and the fact that the workload never becomes simpler or easier are two unfortunate realities that makes being a fifth-grade virtual teacher so nerve-wracking.

This conversation left me with the realization that my struggle would be never-ending. What I had experienced thus far was merely the tip of the iceberg, and what I faced up to this point paled in comparison to the challenges that lay ahead. With an additional five and a half months of the school year still remaining, anything was possible. My adventures would surely continue.